© TIM THOMPSON

SAN ANTONIO
VISIONS

CITYSCAPES
BOOKS

PUBLISHER STEPHEN HUNG

MANAGING EDITOR REGINA ROTHS

ART DIRECTOR AMANDA DAWN GUILMAIN

PROFILE WRITERS LAURIE DOVE, MICHELLE EMERLE, NICK PENA, AND ANDI RODRIGUEZ

SALES MANAGER HENRY HINTERMEISTER

DUST JACKET PHOTOGRAPHER RANDA BISHOP

PAGODA GROUP

BROOKLINE, MASSACHUSETTS

FIRST EDITION
ISBN 978-0-9838481-0-3

PRINTED IN THE UNITED STATES OF AMERICA

Every effort has been made to ensure the accuracy of the information herein. However, the author and Pagoda Group are not responsible for any errors or omissions which might have occurred.

www.cityscapesbooks.com

© TIM THOMPSON

TABLE OF CONTENTS

INTRODUCTION

BY MAYOR JULIÁN CASTRO

© TIM THOMPSON

SAN ANTONIO IS ONE OF THE MOST UNIQUE PLACES IN AMERICA. It is at once one of the most recession-resistant cities in the nation, while also being one of the fastest growing. It is the most popular tourist destination in the state of Texas, while retaining a quality of life more like a friendly small town than a booming metropolitan city. Perhaps most importantly, San Antonio stands out on the American landscape because it has the rare quality of being both a city of history and a city of the future.

Founded in 1718 by the Spanish along a river first settled by Native Americans, San Antonio is today the nation's seventh-largest city and the second-largest city in Texas. The Alamo, the Shrine of Texas Liberty that still symbolizes the epic battle of 1836, is the most visited tourist destination in the state, and is a mere steps away from the famous River Walk.

These are qualities we cherish. But the San Antonio of the 21st century combines that history and character with a populace and cosmopolitan culture that looks like the America of tomorrow. Entrepreneurs, corporations, and marketers are increasingly looking at today's San Antonio to see the American student, worker, and consumer of 2050 and beyond. Home to more than 100,000 college and graduate students, San Antonio is a rising brainpower community. Fortune 500 companies like Valero, Tesoro, USAA, Clear Channel, and NuStar Energy all make their home here. In recent years, they have been joined by cutting-edge biotech and new energy economy companies who are making major investments in San Antonio. The names include companies like Rackspace, Medtronic, InCube Labs, SunEdison, and Consert.

We will always jealously guard the unofficial title of "Military City USA," but we are doing so in cutting-edge ways. Fort Sam Houston, once a major site of basic training for our nation's troops, is now the central training ground for all military medics. Lackland AFB now hosts the 24th Air Force, the cybersecurity command for the entire Air Force which was attracted by the already robust private sector information security network that exists in San Antonio.

People and companies are choosing San Antonio more and more because it is truly unique. Our quality of life hearkens back to an earlier time, and our workforce and business development efforts have positioned us as one of the places to be in the future. In San Antonio, we have the perfect blend of history and vision.

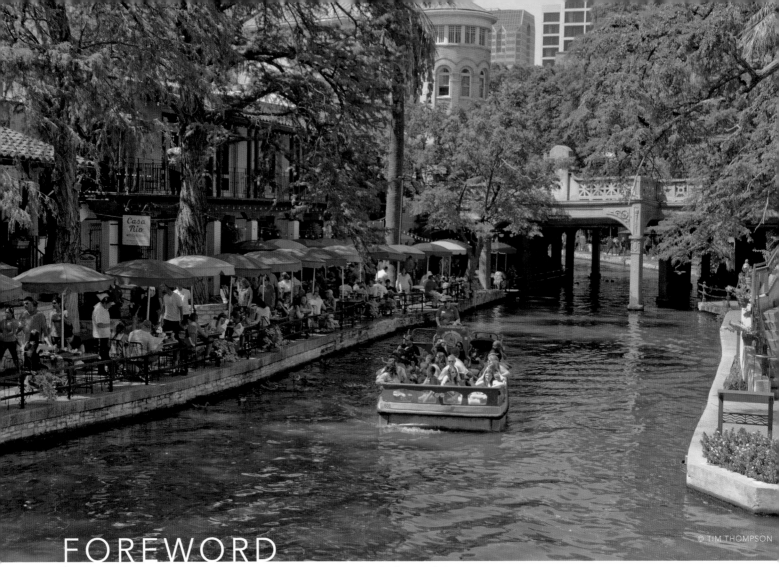

© TIM THOMPSON

FOREWORD

BY HENRY G. CISNEROS

GEOGRAPHERS DESCRIBE THE PLACES ON EARTH where different topographical and ecological zones converge as ecotones. In such places we see unique and notable transitions created by combinations of land features, plant life, and even climates. San Antonio is such a place. It spreads over a landscape that changes even from one part of the city to another. We might even say that the indigenous people who selected the site of the original human settlement many hundreds of years ago selected precisely because it is the place where the hot sand of the brush country to the south transitions into the cool waters that flow from the limestone escarpment to the north. Those indigenous settlers gave the area a name: "Yanaguana." It meant, "The place of the peaceful water."

San Antonio exists at a crossing of landscapes. To the southwest is the brushy coastal savannah, which runs to the Gulf of Mexico and from which migrating Indian tribes gathered food and hunted for perhaps a thousand years before Europeans arrived. Arrayed to the southwest of San Antonio is the hot, arid land where every natural thing seems to bite, sting, prick, or burn. It is the land of cactus, scorpions, and rattlesnakes and it is home to things with descriptive names such as "prickly pears," "poison oak," "horned toads," "fire ants," and "killer bees." It became the domain of legendary ranches and of oil and gas exploration. After trekking up from interior Mexico through this scorching country, Spanish explorers wrote of arriving at the most beautiful oasis they had ever seen. The clear river in the shade of giant cottonwood trees was the edge of what we now call the Texas Hill Country to the northwest, a land of rocky cliffs, cool springs, prevailing breezes, tall oaks, and canyon vistas. To the northeast is the fertile black land that later Texas colonizers, such as Stephen F. Austin, divided into farm sites.

Modern San Antonio has in many ways been shaped by these attributes of the ecotone land over which it has grown. The communities of the Gulf Coast 150 miles to the southeast are modern partners in commerce and recreation. The Port of Corpus Christi is an outlet for goods and products to the world and pristine beaches of the Padre Island National park are the oceanside playground for the entire region. Across an arc ranging to the southwest are working ranches, which give San Antonio its cowboy tradition, as well as the Eagle Ford Shale formation with its prospects for oil and gas production that will rival the Alaskan North Slope over the next twenty years. As a result, the world's leading oil field services companies have located regional headquarters in San Antonio's southern sector.

The Balcones Escarpment to the northwest of San Antonio is a geological formation of caves that make possible the underground limestone aquifer that serves as a reservoir for hundreds of millions of gallons of clear water. San Antonio is the largest city in the nation to draw its water supply from such a source of pure drinking water. The springs and rivers that flow from the Edwards Aquifer — including the San Antonio River — give the city an abundance of parks, flowing creeks, lush tree cover, and flowering plants. The aquifer also provides irrigation for the productive farms that encircle the metropolitan area and sustain the municipal growth that increasingly closes the 75 mile distance to Austin, the nation's fourteenth largest city, with dense urban development along the Austin-San Antonio corridor.

But if geographic features converge to shape a city, then surely the mix of cultural and demographic histories must also influence its character. This is clearly the case in San Antonio. The theme of the city's 1968 World's Fair was "the confluence of cultures," in appreciation of the richness contributed by people of many heritages. Indigenous people first settled here and their pottery shards and arrowheads can still be found at ancient campsites along what is now the world-famous River Walk. Spaniards established five missions beginning in 1691, including the Alamo. The Spanish missions today constitute the only national park of its kind, functioning as historic visitor sites as well as active Catholic parishes. The Spanish created a civilian and military headquarters in San Antonio that governed a territory that stretched to present-day Wyoming, as can be seen on maps in the well-preserved Spanish Governor's Palace across the plaza from the current City Hall.

In 1810 when the Spanish were ejected from Mexico after the Mexican Revolution, San Antonio became part of the new nation of Mexico and remains a major trading partner with Mexico to the present. The Texians, who in 1836 declared the independence of Texas, fought to the last man at the Alamo and prompted the battle cry that would inspire the fight for Texas independence: "Remember the Alamo." From the leaders who drove General Santa Ana

back across the Rio Grande came the civic and business entrepreneurs who made San Antonio the most bustling city in the Lone Star Republic and in the new State of Texas after 1846. They built a city — like New Orleans and San Francisco — that was an innovator in progressive municipal initiatives from gas lamps and street cars to new universities and public parks.

The traditional Texan leadership of San Antonio was defined for a century and a half by the builders of ranching empires, banks, retail stores, oil and gas enterprises, and real estate developments. That leadership cadre was continuously augmented by military officers as San Antonio became home to five major Army and Air Force installations. At various times such legendary names as Douglas MacArthur, Dwight D. Eisenhower, Billy Mitchell, and Charles Lindbergh lived in San Antonio. The city has been enriched by its military heritage and by the leaders who have served or retired here over the years. The interplay of civilian and military history can be seen today in exhibits at the Institute of Texan Cultures in HemisFair Park, at the Briscoe Western Art Museum, at Fort Sam Houston, at the Witte Museum, and at the San Antonio Museum of Art.

The city's original Spanish citizens and later Mexican citizens and the steady stream of immigrants from Mexico, especially after the Mexican Revolution of 1910, gave San Antonio its unique dimension as home to the nation's most prominent and productive Mexican-American community. In truth San Antonio has been much more than a home in the sense of a place of residence; it has become over the years an incubator of institutions of leadership that have advanced the nation's Latino emergence. Here the nation's first Spanish-language radio station — KCOR 1350 AM — was launched. The country's first Spanish language television station — KWEX-TV 41— became the cornerstone of the burgeoning Univision television network. Institutions founded in San Antonio that have propelled national Latino achievements since the 1960s include the Southwest Voter Registration Education Project, the Mexican American Legal Defense and Education Fund, and the Hispanic Association of Colleges and Universities. The nation's first Hispanic elected to Congress was San Antonio's Henry B. Gonzalez and the current mayor, Julian Castro, is respected as a national Hispanic leader. Among the important sites that testify to the city's Hispanic heritage are El Mercado, LaVillita, and the Museo Alameda in downtown, and the Guadalupe Cultural Center in the historic Westside.

Over many decades San Antonio welcomed successive waves of newcomers. Germans escaping religious persecution in their home country established German-speaking churches, schools, labor unions, and benefit organizations. The legacy of German heritage is today visible in the King William neighborhood, at St. Joseph Catholic Church, and at Beethoven Hall with its German choirs and food. Italians populated a near-downtown neighborhood, which is home today to St. Francis de Paola Church and Christopher Columbus Hall, which serves spaghetti dinners on

Sundays. African-Americans settled in San Antonio's Eastside, where they founded thriving newspapers, businesses, and schools, including St. Phillips College. African-American leaders provided critical leadership during the Civil Rights era and helped ease San Antonio's transformation from a city of southern segregation to a city of inclusive collaborative leadership in every sector. The African-American tradition of self-reliant institutions continues today at The Carver Academy, a school founded by NBA superstar David Robinson to combine rigorous academic preparation and spiritually based character development. Poles and Czechs, who had established nearby rural communities with names such as Czestohowa and Panna Maria, concentrated in San Antonio's southeast neighborhoods and brought with them active fraternal societies such as the Sons of Hermann to provide a range of benefits from life insurance to family entertainment. Lebanese, Chinese, Cuban, and Indian immigrants have notably contributed to San Antonio's vitality. Together, this confluence of people and cultures has made modern San Antonio a rich mosaic of ethnic neighborhoods, places of worship, architectural treasures, culinary tastes, musical styles, and family traditions.

The city's population mix continues to be infused by immigration from Mexico, by military postings and retirements in "Military City USA," and by the national pattern of migration to the Sunbelt. Since World War II, San Antonio has evolved into one of the most progressive cities in the nation. Its balanced economy fares well in times of economic downturns and has fueled the city's growth into the seventh most populous city in the U.S. It is an economic engine driven by key military missions, a burgeoning biosciences sector, popular touristic attractions, world-class manufacturing, and an entrepreneurial small business base. A visitor seeking to understand San Antonio's diverse economy could tour Port San Antonio, a massive aerospace industrial park fashioned from the former Kelly Air Force Base; the South Texas Medical Center, the site of more than 49 major medical institutions and 27,000 healthcare professionals; the Toyota Texas Manufacturing plant, which every year produces 200,000 Tundra and Tacoma trucks; and the Henry B. Gonzales Convention Center and the Alamodome, hosts to more than 1,000 conferences and conventions annually.

© TIM THOMPSON

The city's future talent pool is evident in 15 colleges and universities, including branches of Texas' two largest university systems — the University of Texas at San Antonio and Texas A&M University-San Antonio. The five colleges of the Alamo Community College District serve more than 60,000 students. High quality private higher education is available through Trinity University, the University of the Incarnate Word, St. Mary's University, and Our Lady of the Lake University. San Antonio's leaders emphasize education as the unifying theme for building the city's new economy as well as integrating a diverse population.

San Antonio is a city of extraordinary collaboration based on a community consensus about such long-term goals as spurring economic growth to raise incomes, to strengthen the middle class, and to invest in quality education at all levels. Integral to that community consensus is a degree of multicultural respect not evident in many cities. Perhaps because we have lived near each other for so long, we live well together now. The confluence of cultures is real here and has morphed into a unique San Antonio culture that is richer and more fun than the individual parts. Most of us wouldn't live without it. We have learned from the land, we have learned from each other, and now we think we have something to teach the nation.

THE ALAMO is one of five San Antonio missions that served missionaries and their converts in the 1700s. In 1836, with the mission converted to a military post, the Alamo became the site of a crucial battle in the Texas Revolution. Today the Alamo continues to represent a heroic sacrifice for freedom.

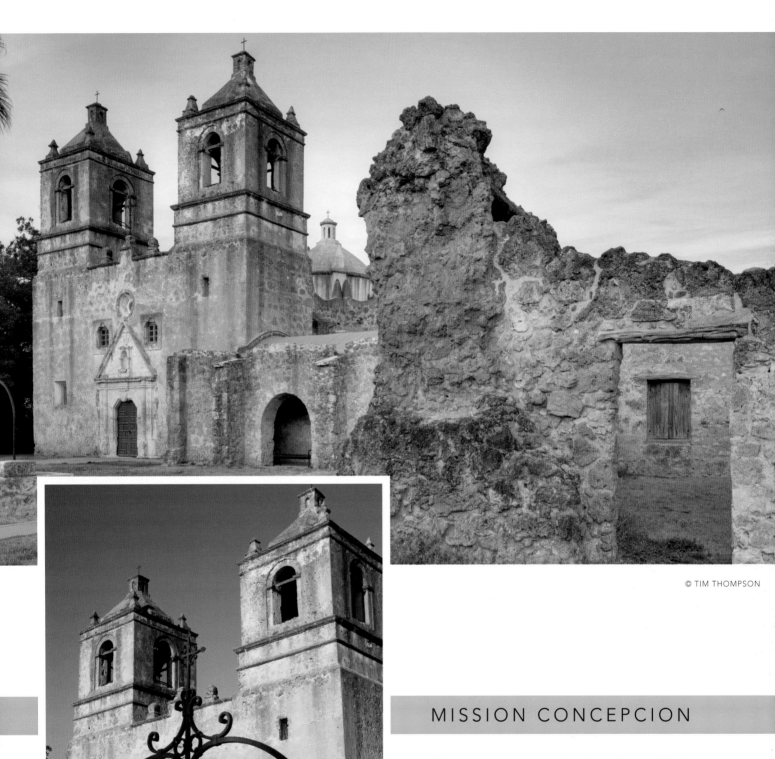

© TIM THOMPSON

© RANDA BISHOP

MISSION CONCEPCION

Mission Nuestra Senora de la Purisima Concepción de Acuna is one of the oldest stone churches in America, erected in the mid-1700s.

© TIM THOMPSON

© TIM THOMPSON

© RANDA BISHOP

MISSION SAN JOSE

Mission San Jose was a cultural center, serving as home to hundreds who raised crops and livestock. The mission's dramatic Spanish Colonial architecture remains largely intact since the structure's construction in 1720.

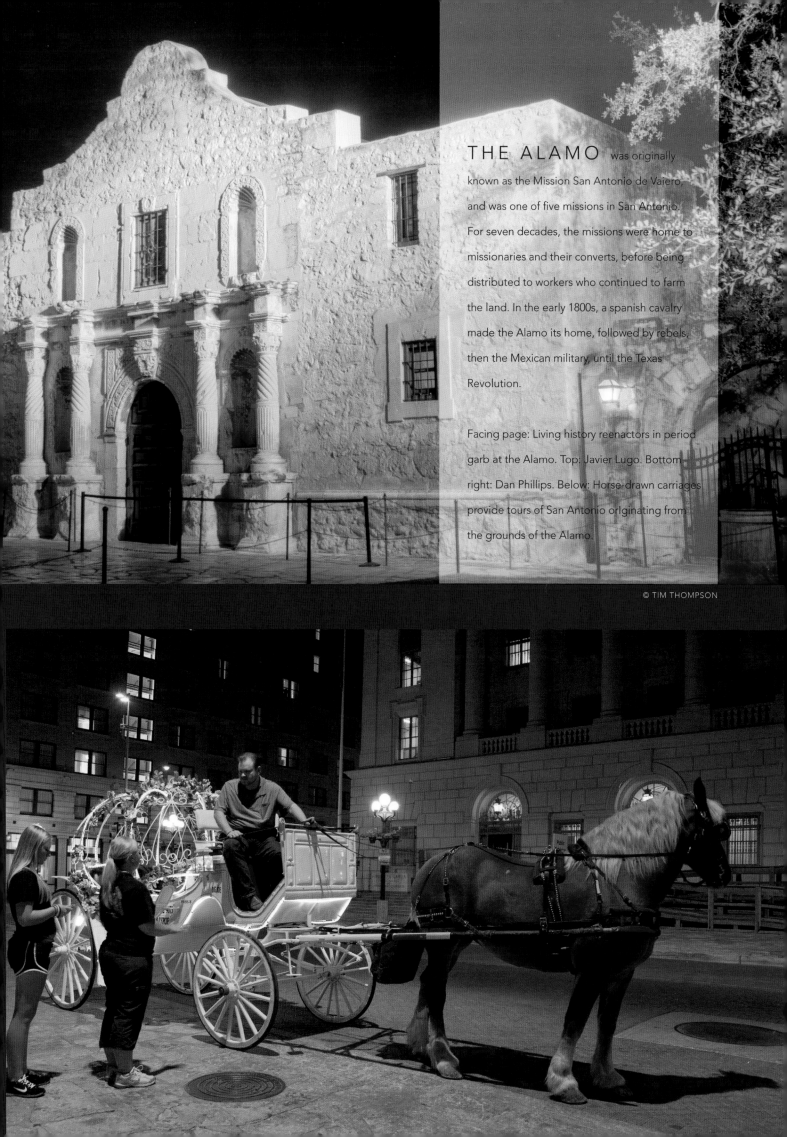

THE ALAMO was originally known as the Mission San Antonio de Valero, and was one of five missions in San Antonio. For seven decades, the missions were home to missionaries and their converts, before being distributed to workers who continued to farm the land. In the early 1800s, a spanish cavalry made the Alamo its home, followed by rebels, then the Mexican military, until the Texas Revolution.

Facing page: Living history reenactors in period garb at the Alamo. Top: Javier Lugo. Bottom right: Dan Phillips. Below: Horse-drawn carriages provide tours of San Antonio originating from the grounds of the Alamo.

© TIM THOMPSON

MISSION SAN JUAN

Mission San Juan Capistrano was moved from
East Texas to the banks of the San Antonio
River in 1731.

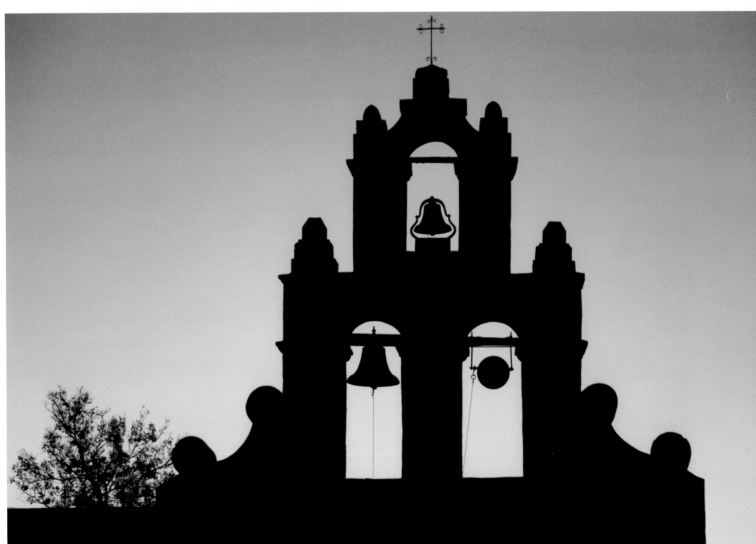

© RANDA BISHOP

© RANDA BISHOP

MISSION ESPADA

Mission San Francisco de la Espada,
the southernmost of the five missions
on the San Antonio River, began in East
Texas and moved to its current location
in 1731.

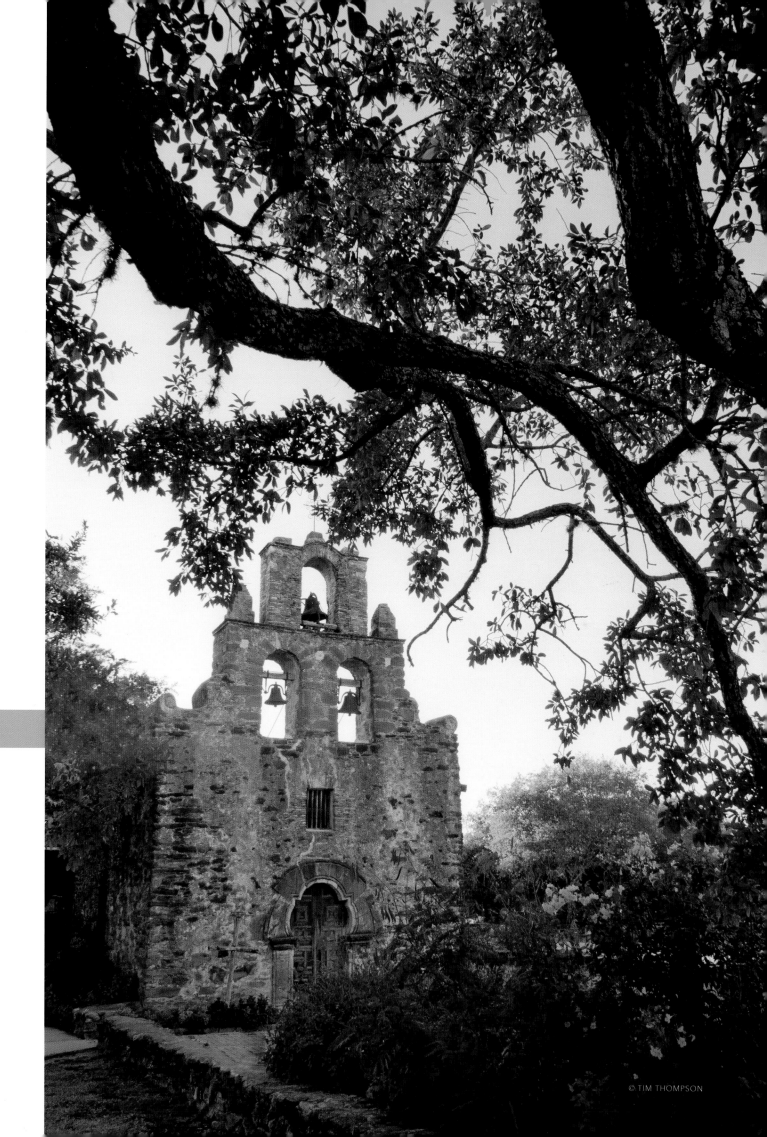

© TIM THOMPSON

© RANDA BISHOP

MARIACHI MASSES take place each week in San Antonio at Mission San Jose and San Fernando Cathedral.

FLAMENCO can be found at venues throughout San Antonio. Facing page: top and bottom right: Flamenco dancers perform during a production of "Pasos y Pasiones" ("Steps and Passions") at the Cameo Theatre as part of Flamenco Fest, sponsored by the San Antonio Parks and Recreation Department. Facing page, lower left: Carmens de la Calle Cafe has flamenco dancers on Friday nights. This page: Renowned flamenco dancer and director of the Fandango Youth Ensemble Sonia Jimenez, led and choreographed dancers at Flamenco Fest.

© RANDA BISHOP

© RANDA BISHOP

© RANDA BISHOP

INSTRUCTOR Mona Lisa Montgomery teaches students at the Berta Almaguer Dance Studio in the use of castanuelas (castanets). This class is a program through San Antonio Parks and Recreation.

© TIM THOMPSON

© TIM THOMPSON

THE ALAMO CENOTAPH

is a 60-foot-tall memorial to those who died defending the mission.

© TIM THOMPSON

© TIM THOMPSON

THE 750-FOOT-TALL
TOWER OF THE AMERICAS

was built for the 1968 World's Fair, which celebrated San Antonio's 250th Anniversary. The tower houses a revolving restaurant and an observation deck, where visitors can enjoy breathtaking views of the city.

© TIM THOMPSON

© RANDA BISHOP

© TIM THOMPSON

© TIM THOMPSON

© TIM THOMPSO

TORCH OF FRIENDSHIP

The 65-foot-tall Torch of Friendship was created by sculptor

Sebastian at the request of the Mexican entrepreneurs'

association as a gift to the people of San Antonio.

© RANDA BISHOP

© RANDA BISHOP

© RANDA BISHOP

SEPTEMBER 16 marks Mexico's independence from Spain and San Antonio celebrates with numerous activities, including a colorful parade complete with marching bands like this one (left) from John Jay High School. Below: Members of the military and (facing page) an ROTC competition were also part of Diez y Seis (September 16) events.

© RANDA BISHOP

© RANDA BISHOP

DIEZ Y SEIS, celebrating Mexico's independence from Spain, events include a parade. Top: A mariachi band plays on one of the floats. Left: Gerardo "Jerry" Diaz was grand marshall of the 2011 parade. Above: Our Lady of Guadalupe Church Senior Center King and Queen.

A national landmark,

THE SPANISH GOVERNOR'S PALACE is the former home and office of the Presidio San Antonio de Bejar. Carvings in the front door of the palace relate the history of Spanish America.

© RANDA BISHOP

FIVE & DIME
SPURS
SOUVENIR
T-SHIRTS
$19.99

PROPERTY OF
SAN ANTONIO
SPURS
N ANTONI

Medium
Medium

© RANDA BISHOP

© RANDA BISHOP

© TIM THOMPSON

NIGHTLIFE IN SAN ANTONIO includes music and dance, the likes of (clockwise from top right) performances like The Musical Magic of George & Ira Gershwin Fascinating Rhythm at the Cameo Theatre, Harry Brun and the Latin Playerz, and the high school jazz band "Take Note" at Bravo Latino jazz night at the Arneson Theatre in La Villita along the San Antonio River.

LA CHIQUITA

— a family owned panaderias in San Antonio's Westside neighborhood — specializes in homede pan dulce.

Mother Leticia, and daughter Gabriella, with a pan of freshly baked goods.

NIKI'S TOKYO INN features

traditional sushi and Japanese favorites.

MARKET SQUARE is a three-block-long outdoor plaza lined with shops and restaurants like the family owned Mi Tierra Café y Panaderia.

JAPANESE
TEA GARDEN

© TIM THOMPSON

© RANDA BISHOP

THE SAN ANTONIO BOTANICAL GARDEN

encompasses 38 acres of beauty and includes

formal beds, a native plant trail, a conservatory,

special exhibits, a bistro, and more.

Bernardo Balestrieri, *Boy with Fish Basket*

COLLECTIONS

at the McNay Art Museum include 19th- through 21st-century European and American works, the Tobin Collection of Theatre Arts, and Medieval & Renaissance art. Left: "Ascent," by Alexander Liberman, purchased with the Russell Hill Rogers Fund for the Arts.

THE KING WILLIAM
DISTRICT was San Antonio's most elegent
address in the late 1800s. The 25-block area is near
downtown on the south bank of the San Antonio River.

THE STEVES HOMESTEAD

is an elegant, three-story mansion built in 1876 for lumber

magnate Edward Steves.

© RANDA BISHOP

A DINNER BOAT CRUISE on the San Antonio River may include a glimpse of the Ballet Folklorico Festival at the Arneson Theater in La Villita.

© RANDA BISHOP

© RANDA BISHOP

© RANDA BISHOP

SAN FERNANDO CATHEDRAL

© RANDA BISHOP

THE LITTLE CHURCH OF LA VILLITA, circa

1879 (above and right). Facing page, top: Mustang Grey's is one of the La Villita area's many eclectic shops.

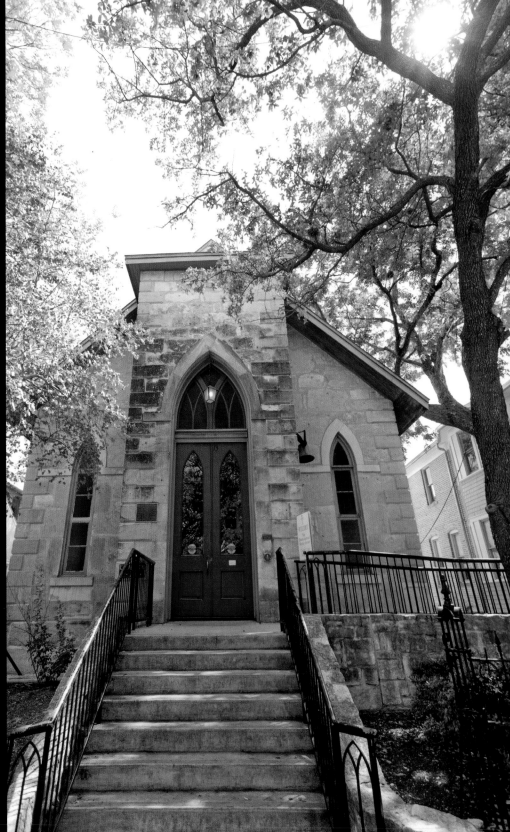

© TIM THOMPSON

© TIM THOMPSON

© RANDA BISHOP

OVER TIME, THE LA VILLITA area has

been home to Spanish soldiers stationed at the Alamo, German and French

immigrants who became city movers and shakers, and an area of decline that

has seen a renaissance to become a colorful and thriving art community.

© TIM THOMPSON

© RANDA BISHOP

THE CENTRAL LIBRARY of the San Antonio Public Library is a work of art all its own. Designed by

renowned Mexican architect Ricardo Legorreta Vilchis, the building is noted for its striking color, locally referred to as "Enchilada Red."

Right: "Comprando y Prestando" by Mary Helen Herrera. Bottom: "Roots of Change" by Adriana Garcia.

© RANDA BISHOP

© RANDA BISHOP

ARTIST
JESSE TREVINO

JESSE TREVINO'S murals are distinctive landmarks that reflect the culture of the community. Right: "La Veladora" (candle) of Our Lady of Guadalupe is a three-dimensional, 40-foot-tall mosaic on the side of the Guadalupe Cultural Arts Center building, which was dedicated to victims of the 9/11 attacks. Above: "Spirit of Healing," is a 90-foot-tall ceramic tile mosaic on the side of the Christus Santa Rosa Children's Hospital.

THE CULINARY INSTITUTE OF AMERICA

, San Antonio, has an associate degree program for students interested in the culinary arts. The college also offers a Latin Cuisines Certificate Program that delves into both food and culture. Overlooking the teaching kitchen is the CIA Bakery Café, which offers sandwiches, soups, salads, and delectable pastries. Right: Chef Cynthia Keller (far right) provides instruction.

© RANDA BISHOP

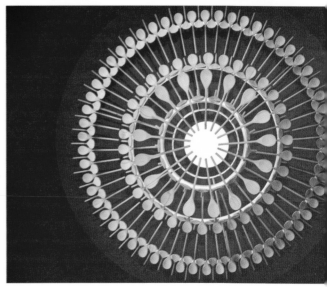

© RANDA BISHOP

THE FRESHEST
WARES can be found at San

Antonio farmer's markets.

© RANDA BISHOP

© RANDA BISHOP

© RANDA BISHOP

WHATEVER YOUR TASTES, San Antonio's eateries are sure to satisfy your hunger and quench your thirst. Texas-sized favorites include (clockwise from left, facing page) a warm welcome at the Republic of Texas restaurant, drinks and appetizers at Barriba Cantina, dessert at Schilo's Delicatessen, a Texas-shaped waffle at the Hotel Indigo's 1909 Bar and Bistro, and a plate of paella and Carmens de la Calle Café owner Paula Sullivan with a pitcher of her special sangria.

© TIM THOMPSON

© RANDA BISHOP

THE GUENTHER HOUSE is the

home of Pioneer Flour Mills' founding family. The property

includes the family's restored 1860 home, an award-winning

restaurant, the River Mill Store, and space for special events.

© RANDA BISHOP

IN 1991, Gov. Ann Richards made the square dance the official state folk dance of Texas. Today, clubs like the Grand Squares and Come N' Take It let you do-si-do. Above: Janet Abell with her father Charles Macha. Below: Wiley and Charlene Berryman.

© RANDA BISHOP

© RANDA BISHOP

© TIM THOMPSON

WHETHER IT'S live music, line dancing, or dinner and drinks,

San Antonio's nightlife has something for everyone. Above and right: Weekend

jazz at Olmos Bharmacy. Facing page, top: Renowned Tejano music accordionist

Leonardo "Flaco" Jimenez.

SAN ANTONIO has a swingin' jazz scene, with annual festivals and a host of venues featuring live acts. Below: Joey DeFrancisco at Jazz'SAlive. Facing page: Mindi Abair at Balcones Heights Jazz Festival.

© TIM THOMPSON

THE STRIKING BEXAR COUNTY COURTHOUSE building is an example of a

Romanesque Revival. Designed by J. Riely Gordon and built in the 1890s,

the building was added to the National Register of Historic Places in the

1970s and now serves as the county seat of Bexar County.

© RANDA BISHOP

THERE ARE A NUMBER

of interesting ways to traverse San Antonio and see the sights.

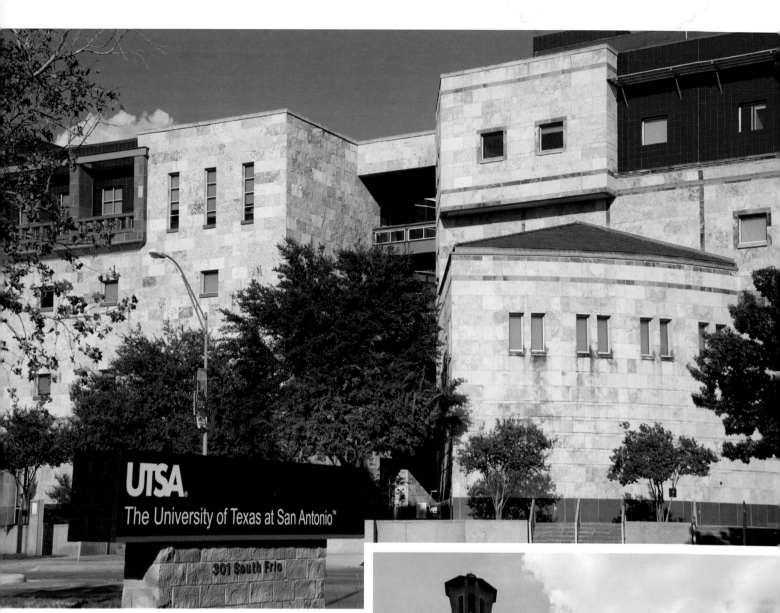

© RANDA BISHOP

SAN ANTONIO is home to a number of institutes of higher learning, including San Antonio College, Our Lady of the Lake University, St. Mary's University, the University of Texas at San Antonio (above), Texas A&M University-San Antonio, Trinity University (right), University of the Incarnate Word (opposite page), University of Texas at San Antonio, and Wayland Baptist University.

© TIM THOMPSON

ALAMO ST.

Rio Taxi

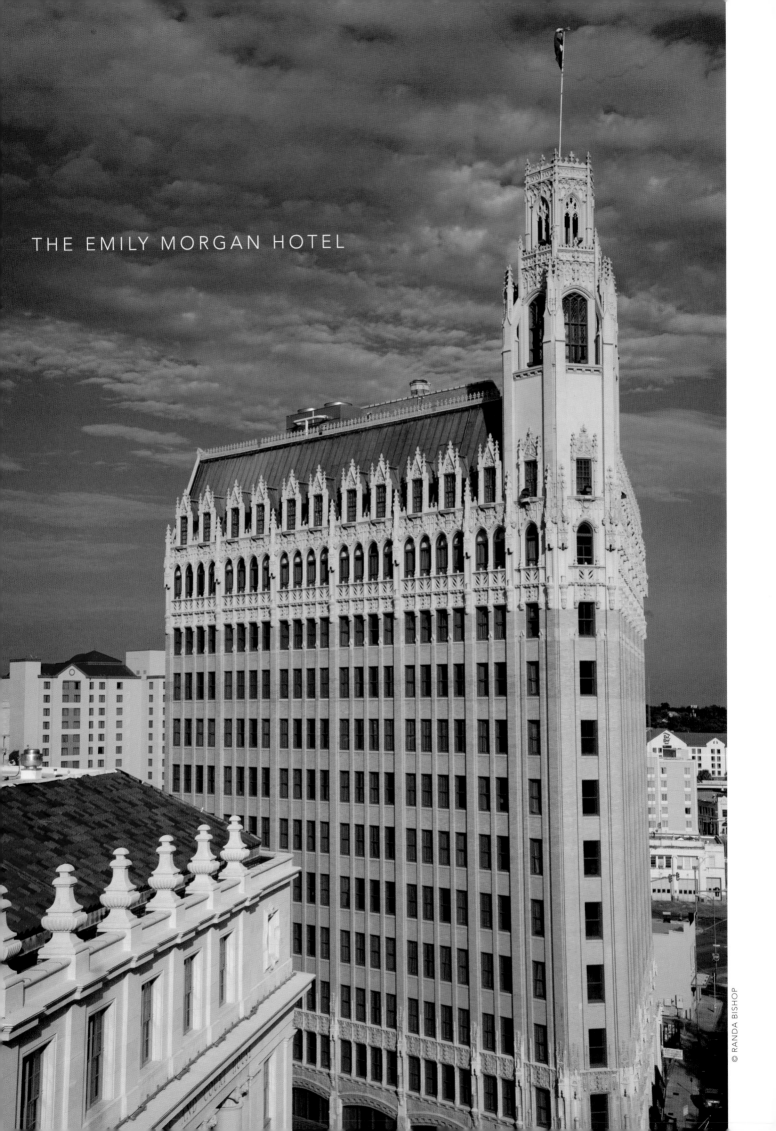

THE EMILY MORGAN HOTEL

THE TOWER LIFE
BUILDING

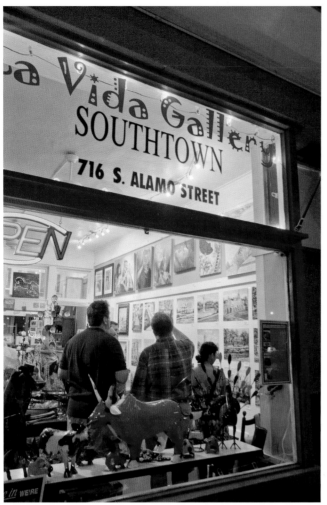

© TIM THOMPSON

© TIM THOMPSON

FIRST FRIDAYS in Southtown (the area just south of downtown) are a celebration of the local arts scene.

© TIM THOMPSON

"HIGH HAIR AND JALAPENOS," a comedy satirizing all things Texan, played at the Cameo Theatre. The venue, with its Egyptian Art Deco décor, has hosted some of the biggest names in entertainment and continues to delight audiences with everything from films and plays to concerts and parties.

THE MUSEO ALAMEDA was inspired

by a nearby theater, which was the brainchild of renowned boot

company icon, G.A. Lucchese. The museum is now an affiliate of

the Smithsonian in Washington, D.C. and a national center for

Latino arts and culture. Above: "Casa Moreles in Memory" by

Artist Franco Mondini-Ruiz is an installation inspired by botanica

stores, which sell folk-healing merchandise like candles, potions,

medicinal herbs, and religious icons. Left: Wooden Italian

carousel horse painted by Jesus "Chucho" Reyes Ferreira.

ONCE THRIVING SAN ANTONIO BUSINESSES are seeing new life as mixed-use developments. The Pearl Brewery Complex is now a collection of shops, restaurants, cultural amenities, and more. The Lone Star Brewing Co. building houses the San Antonio Museum of Art. The Aztec Theatre is home to shops and the "San Antonio Rose Live" country music show.

© TIM THOMPSON

© RANDA BISHOP

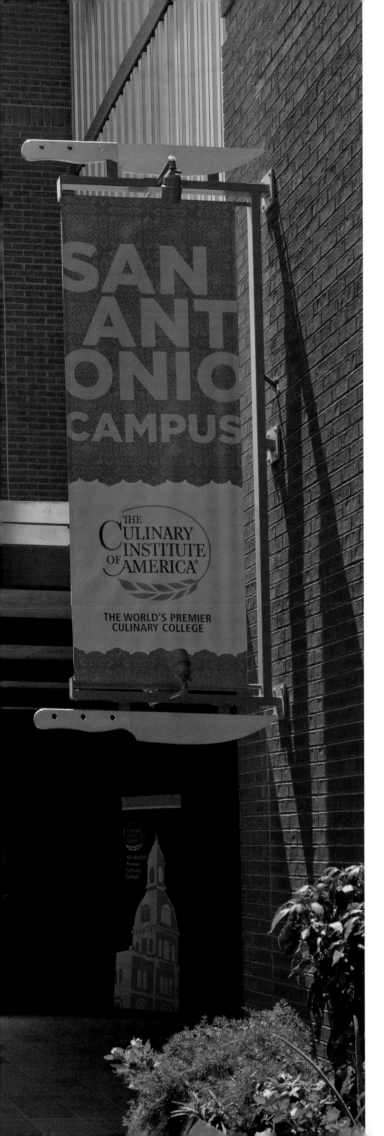

AN ALAMO
RANGER

handles the distinctive

state flag.

© TIM THOMPSON

THE JOHNSON STREET BRIDGE

— a pedestrian bridge crossing the
San Antonio River — is affectionately
known as the O. Henry bridge
because the famed author included
the structure in some of his stories.
San Antonio was the setting for several
O. Henry stories. Right: The author
lived in this house in 1885.

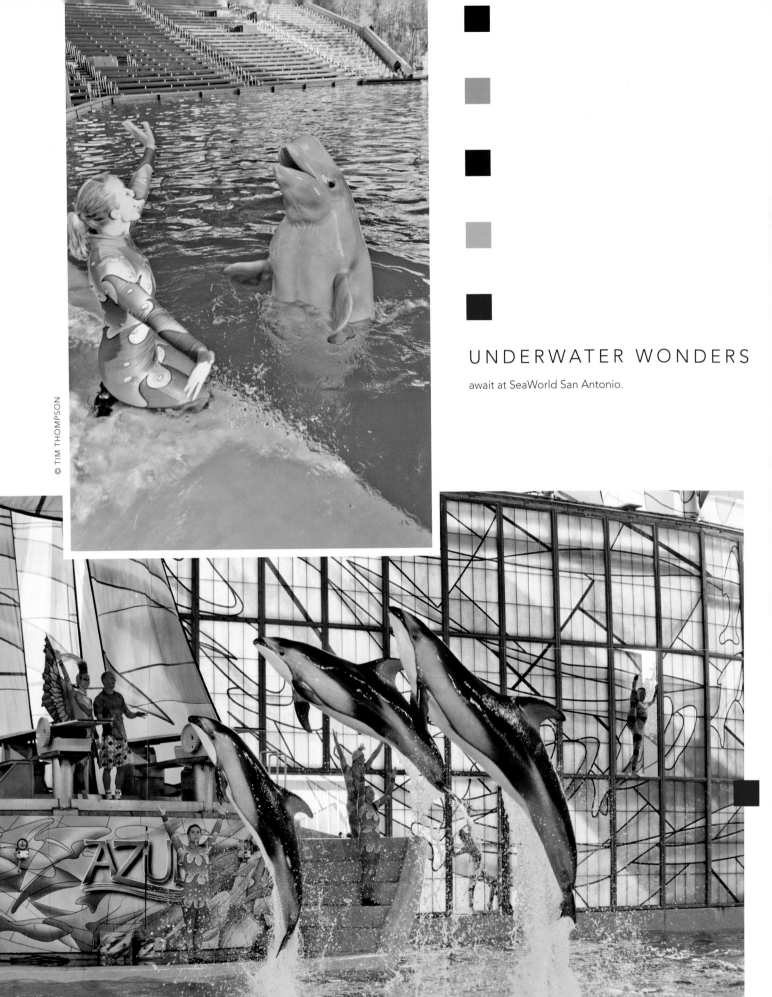

© TIM THOMPSON

UNDERWATER WONDERS

await at SeaWorld San Antonio.

© TIM THOMPSON

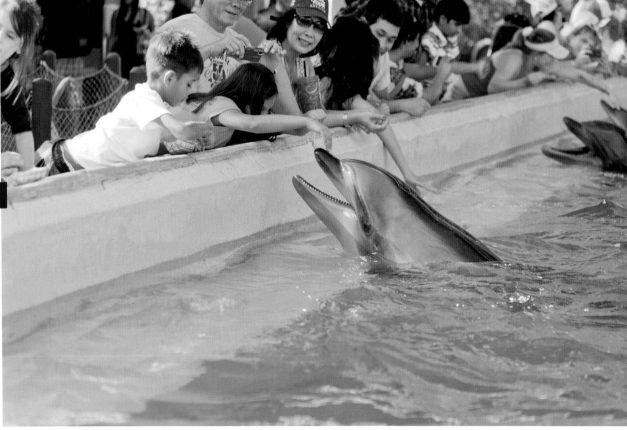

© TIM THOMPSON

© TIM THOMPSON

© TIM THOMPSON

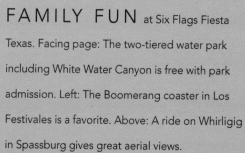

FAMILY FUN at Six Flags Fiesta

Texas. Facing page: The two-tiered water park including White Water Canyon is free with park admission. Left: The Boomerang coaster in Los Festivales is a favorite. Above: A ride on Whirligig in Spassburg gives great aerial views.

SWEET SIXTE

sisters in the gardens of the M

Art Museum.

WOODLAWN LAKE PARK

THE SHOPS
AT LA
CANTERA

all decked out for the

holidays.

© RUDY ORNELAS

© RUDY ORNELAS

© TIM THOMPSON

THE MELISSA GUERRA SHOP specializes in

Latin American kitchen implements and hard-to-find cooking ingredients.

© TIM THOMPSON

SAN ANTONIO is a bicycle-friendly town and visitors can enjoy the sights on their own or as part of guided tours.

GLASS ARTIST GINI GARCIA (below) oversees the fabrication of her designs at her glass blowing studio. Garcia's works can be found in residences and commercial properties throughout San Antonio and at her Gallery on the River Walk.

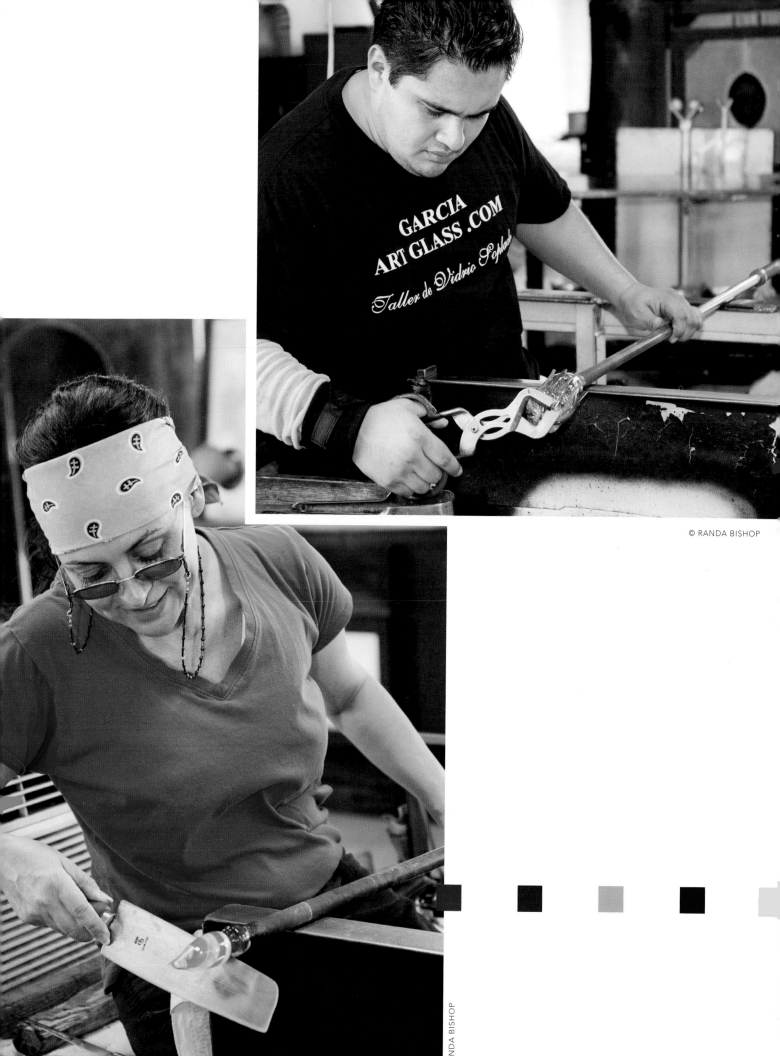

© RANDA BISHOP

© RANDA BISHOP

© RUDY ORNELAS

© RANDA BISHOP

AFFECTIONATELY KNOWN as "The Giant Justins," these 40-foot-tall cowboy boots sit at the entrance to North Star Mall. The boots were created by artist Bob "Daddy-O" Wade (below) and installed in 1980.

© RUDY ORNELAS

WHEN FOLKS IN SAN ANTONIO

want a little getaway, they often head for the Texas Hill Country, a place of beautiful natural wonder.

© CARRIE YONLEY

© CARRIE YONLEY

© CARRIE YONLEY

YOU'LL KNOW you're in cowboy country when you arrive at Bandera, Texas. Located in the Texas Hill Country just northwest of San Antonio, Bandera is known as the Cowboy Capital of the World.

© TIM THOMPSON

COMPACT
CAR
PARKING
ONLY

e realty.com   830.796.4

© TIM THOMPSON

FOR AN AUTHENTIC cowboy experience, head on over to Bandera. The county is known for its rodeos, including the annual Labor Day Weekend celebration complete with longhorn cattle drive, parade, arts and crafts fair, re-enactors, and more.

© TIM THOMPSON

THE ANNUAL

Celebrate Bandera festival, in Bandera, Texas, has included the Circle of Life Intertribal Powwow.

© RANDA BISHOP

A FLAG CEREMONY opens the Gran Charreada (rodeo) at the Diaz Ranch near New Braunfels. Below: Charro Gerardo "Jerry" Diaz shows his amazing roping skills. Bottom photo: A bull rider hits the arena.

© RANDA BISHOP

© RANDA BISHOP

ESCARAMUZA SIDESADDLE riders Margarita

Medina and daughter Jasmin, at right. Above: Staci Anderson-Diaz rides a

foursome of beautiful Azteca horses.

© RANDA BISHOP

SINCE 1878, folks have been coming to Gruene Hall, Texas' oldest dance hall, located in New Braunfels. Above: Erik Hokkanen and the Flat Top Band.

© RANDA BISHOP

© RANDA BISHOP

© CARRIE YONLEY

TEXAS WILDFLOWERS

© CARRIE YONLEY

EVERY YEAR, more than one million visitors stop in to see the residents of the San Antonio Zoo and Aquarium. The 56-acre zoo is home to more than 3,500 animals representing some 600 species. The zoo is open every day of the year.

© RANDA BISHOP

© RANDA BISHOP

NATURAL BRIDGE WILDLIFE
RANCH, just north of San Antonio near New Braunfels, has both
native and exotic animals who will step right up to your vehicle for a bite of
food, which is supplied by the facility as part of a self-drive tour.

© RANDA BISHOP

© RANDA BISHOP

© RANDA BISHOP

© RANDA BISHOP

© RANDA BISHOP

OPENED IN 1993, the Alamodome is a $186 million, 1.6 million-square-foot facility that is owned and operated by the City of San Antonio.

© RANDA BISHOP

© RANDA BISHOP

© RANDA BISHOP

THE FORT SAM HOUSTON

National Historic Landmark comprises the Department of
Defense's largest collection of historic buildings. The post
now serves as the "Home of Military Medicine," with medical,
dental, and veterinary units among its tenants.

© RANDA BISHOP

THE 341ST TRAINING SQUADRON at Lackland Air Force Base oversees the Military Working Dog Program, which trains dogs for use in patrol, detection of drugs and explosives, and specialized missions for the Department of Defense.

© RANDA BISHOP

© RANDA BISHO

© RANDA BISHOP

PROUD
PARENTS and

family members attend the

Air Force Basic Training

graduation.

© RANDA BISHOP

© RANDA BISHOP

© RANDA BISHOP

LACKLAND AIR FORCE BASE,

Texas, is part of the 502nd Air Base Wing. The base is home to more

the 37th Training Wing, which is the largest training wing in the U.S.

Air Force.

THE MISSING MAN MONUMENT is

an aluminum and steel sculpture by artist Mark Pritchett, which symbolizes the U.S. Air Force Thunderbird Aerial Team's formation paying homage to fallen soldiers.

NICKNAMED THE
TAJ MAHAL, the Randolph
Air Force Base Building 100 houses the
headquarters for the 12th Flying Training

ALAMO RANGER
J. HOOD.

A SAN ANTONIO
AMBASSADOR known

as an Alamo Amigo.

SAN ANTONIO'S FINEST participate in the Diez y Seis (September 16) parade celebrating Mexico's independence from Spain.

THE TERRELL HILLS FIRE DEPARTMENT protects citizens in this San Antonio suburb.

© TIM THOMPSON

"THE VIRGIN OF GUADALUPE," an 18th century oil on canvas at the center of a carved gilded altar.

© RANDA BISHOP

THE SAN ANTONIO MUSEUM OF ART, affectionately known as "SAM."

© RANDA BISHOP

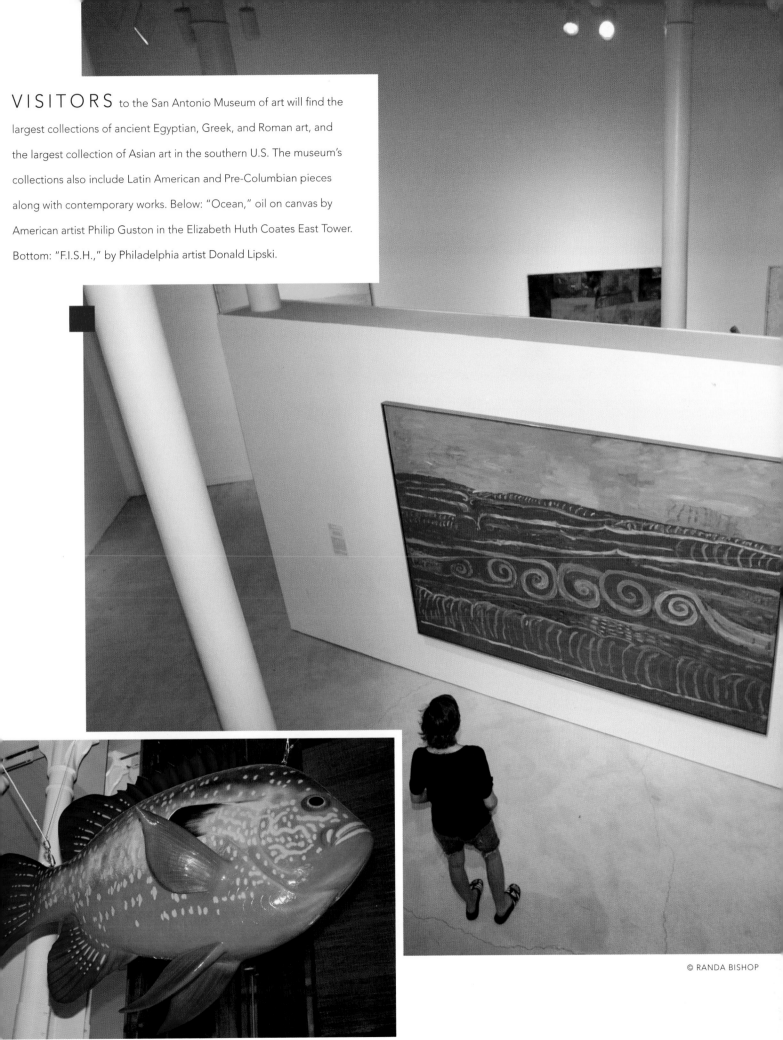

VISITORS to the San Antonio Museum of art will find the largest collections of ancient Egyptian, Greek, and Roman art, and the largest collection of Asian art in the southern U.S. The museum's collections also include Latin American and Pre-Columbian pieces along with contemporary works. Below: "Ocean," oil on canvas by American artist Philip Guston in the Elizabeth Huth Coates East Tower. Bottom: "F.I.S.H.," by Philadelphia artist Donald Lipski.

© RANDA BISHOP

© RANDA BISHOP

THE SAN ANTONIO CHILDREN'S MUSEUM

is three floors of interactive exhibits for kids. Below and facing page: In PowerBall Hall, balls fed into a variety of mechanisms fill an elevated ball drop. Bottom photo: Milking "Alamoo." Right: Science City brings out the scientist in a kid.

© RANDA BISHOP

© RANDA BISHOP

© RANDA BISHOP

© RANDA BI

© RANDA BISHOP

LOCATED on the University of Texas San Antonio HemisFair Park Campus, in downtown San Antonio, the Institute of Texan Cultures is 65,000-square-feet of displays and interactive exhibits that provide cultural insight into all that was and is Texas.

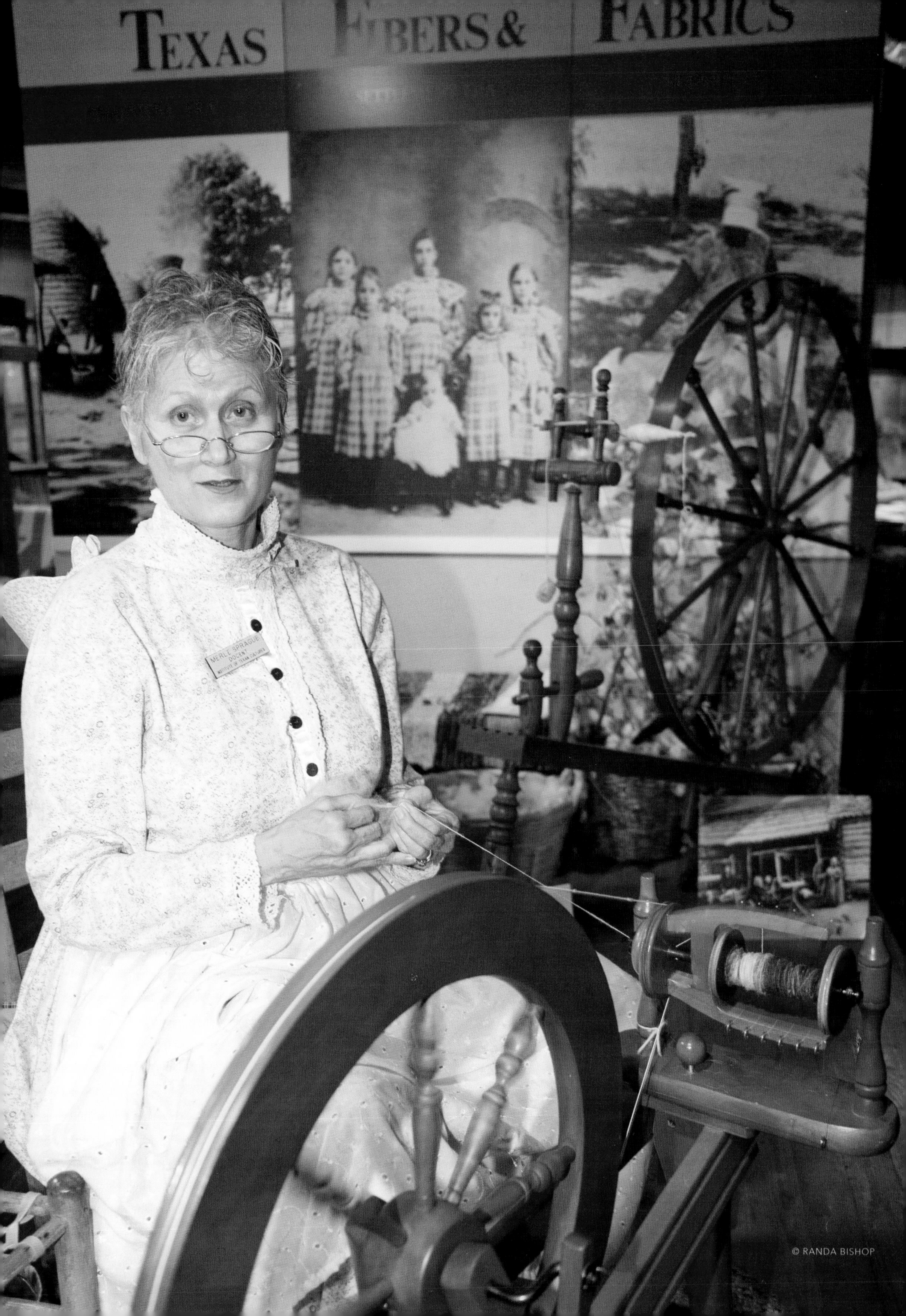

© RANDA BISHOP

DISPLAYS at the Institute of Texan Cultures cover the multitude of cultures that inhabit Texas. Below: A two-room sharecropper's house from the early 1900s. Facing page, top: A mural of Native American life.

"TEXAS BOB" REINHARDT at the Buckhorn

Saloon & Museum and The Texas Ranger
Museum, encompassing two museums, a café, a
gift shop, and a shooting gallery.

© TIM THOMPSON

© TIM THOMPSON

THE WITTE MUSEUM features

exhibits and programs on

natural history, science, and the

heritage of South Texas.

SAN ANTONIO
MAYOR JULIÁ
CASTRO (top photo,
left) and his twin brother, State
Rep. Joaquin Castro, D-San
Antonio. When elected in 2009
Julián Castro was the youngest
mayor ever of a Top 50 America
city. Café College, one of Mayo
Castro's initiatives, offers free
guidance for San Antonians
looking to enter college.

SOUTHERN PACIFIC locomotive

#794. Right: The Depot is part of the restored Sunset Station, a train depot converted into an event facility in the St. Paul Square historic district.

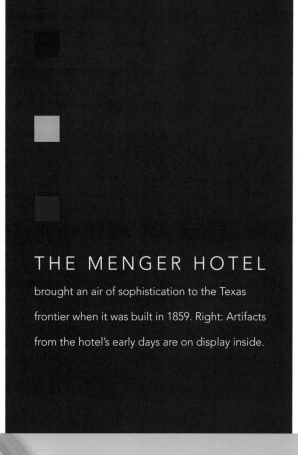

THE MENGER HOTEL

brought an air of sophistication to the Texas

frontier when it was built in 1859. Right: Artifacts

from the hotel's early days are on display inside.

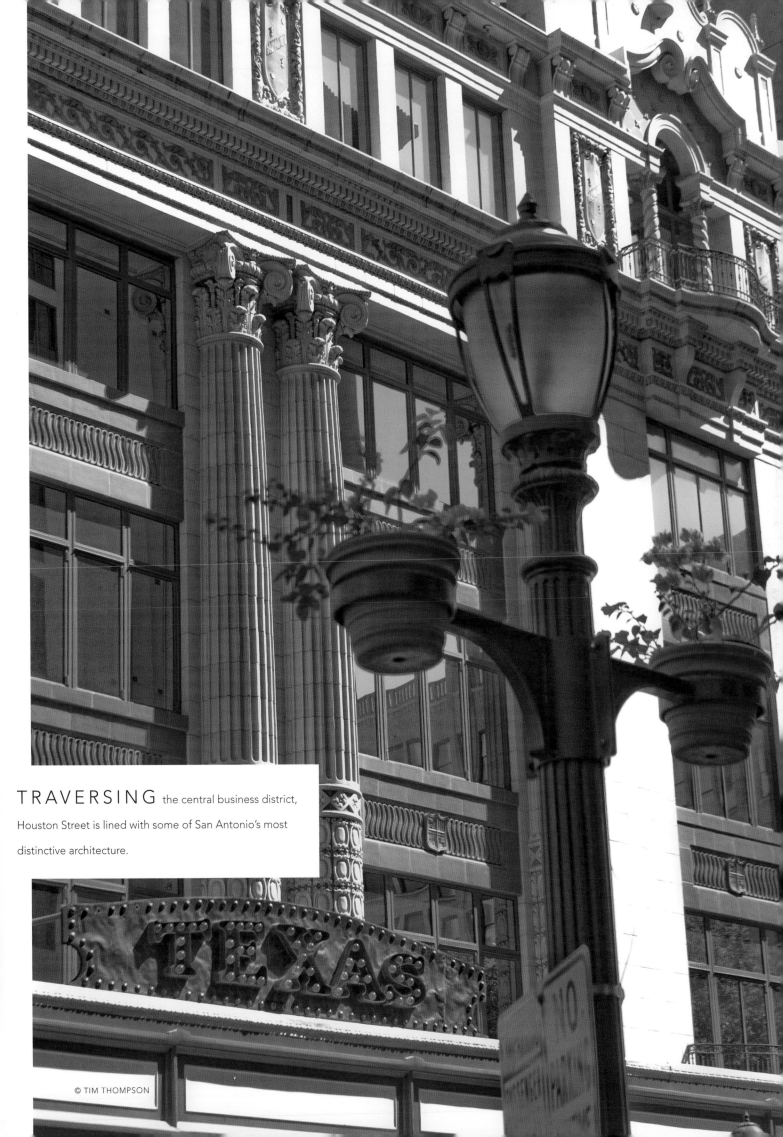

TRAVERSING the central business district, Houston Street is lined with some of San Antonio's most distinctive architecture.

ST. JOSEPH CATHOLIC CHURCH, built in 1868, is encircled by the Rivercenter Mall.

SAN
FERNANDO
CATHEDRAL
AT NIGHT

SAN ANTONIO SYMPHONY in the Main Plaza

ROYALTY COINS

PROFILES IN EXCELLENCE

BRONZE STATUE atop the copper dome of the VIA Metropolitan Westside Multimodal Transit Center, which encompasses a bus rapid transit terminal and access to Amtrak, intercity bus service, and taxis.

C.H. GUENTHER & SON, INC.

IN 1848, A RESOURCEFUL AND DETERMINED young German immigrant, 22-year-old Carl Hilmar Guenther, set out to make his way to America, "the land of opportunity." The steadfastness, foresight, and careful endeavors of this young man would produce a respected maker of flour and cornmeal products, gravies and baking mixes, as well as seasoning mixes and frozen foods that would thrive well into a second century of operation.

Born in the Prussian province of Saxony, Guenther was the third of eight children and the eldest son of well-to-do cloth merchants. When C.H. Guenther arrived in America, he spent two years working as a laborer before heading for Texas, where he heard flour milling was in short supply.

Recognizing the opportunity that lay before him, Guenther boldly wrote his father asking for his $2,000 inheritance, and in 1851 he constructed a mill near the juncture of the Pedernales River and Live Oak Creek in Fredericksburg.

Guenther's mill was perfectly timed as it relieved residents of the thriving German settlement the tedious daily task of grinding their own grain by hand. Early spring 1855, Guenther married a local girl, 16-year-old Dorothea Wilhelmine Henriette Pape, and within four years the couple's family had grown by two.

Late in 1859, Guenther again seized the opportunity that lay before him and headed for the bustling city of San Antonio, population some 8,200, where he constructed a steam-operated flour mill on the San Antonio River. This technology would handle more grain than the area was currently producing. Taking a chance, Guenther convinced local farmers to plant more wheat than they ever had before because his new steam-powered mill would quickly grind it all. With that promise, Guenther, then 33, successfully laid the foundation of his future and those of his descendants.

By 1868 the company had added ice manufacturing to its operations and the birth of a seventh child, Erhard, completed C.H. Guenther's family. Consumer demand dictated the need for a second mill, which was built a couple of miles upstream. By 1877, as technology progressed, Guenther switched oxen transport to the railway that now connected San Antonio with the rest of the nation. Guenther was able to double the size of his original mill and add a turbine wheel that, at capacity in a single day, could put out enough barrels of flour to fill the needs of the entire city!

The company operated as C.H. Guenther & Sons from 1878 until 1894, when second son Arthur opened his own mill just two miles north of his father's mill. This decision caused the elder Guenther to immediately remove "Sons" from the company business, but C.H. Guenther & Son soon was more commonly promoted as Pioneer Flour Mills in a nod to the company's most popular brand — Pioneer. In an effort to avoid confusion with the son's competing mill, Carl Hilmar Guenther added his iconic bearded image to every barrelhead and sack produced. By 1898, only youngest son Erhard and his father continued on in the business, nurturing the strong and enterprising roots still evident today, more than a century and a half later.

Of the many challenges C. H. Guenther successfully battled over time, competition was just one. The company has survived depressed economic conditions, supply shortages resulting from wars and drought, floods, renovations, untimely deaths, and the challenge of new technologies.

Throughout the years, continued brand recognition has proven to be a strong factor for C. H. Guenther & Son, Inc. Names like Pioneer, White Wings, Morrison, Williams, and SunBird have become household words, popularized by sheer product quality as well as innovative marketing strategies ranging from billboard parade floats to televised cooking shows.

Strategic diversification has also proven to be a key to the company's success. In addition to constructing better facilities and implementing new technologies, the company added to its product lineup convenient baking mixes, frozen foods, ready-to-eat flour tortillas, and a white gravy mix that would quickly become — and has successfully remained — a best seller. Continued research and development for innovative products has brought about such items as the well-known McDonald's McGriddle.

The company's physical property's dynamics have also grown over time through new construction and acquisitions. In 2002, the company expanded its frozen and dry mix operations to a third site in Prosperity, S.C. Prior to that, in 1987, the company made its first acquisition with the purchase of Texas Custom Bakers, a frozen foods company, and in the mid-90s, the company acquired the iconic White Lily Foods Company of Knoxville, Tenn. Other acquisitions have included Golden West Bakeries from RHM Ltd., serving the United Kingdom and Belgium; Morrison Milling Company of Denton, Texas, a long-time grain-product manufacturer; Williams Foods of Lenexa, Kan., a producer of dry seasonings and mixes; and Trousdale Bakery Ltd., a bun producer near London, England.

In 1982 management of the company passed to a non-family member for the first time. Today C.H. Guenther & Son, Inc. proudly holds the title of being the oldest, continuously operated, family-owned milling company in the United States.

The Guenther House, former home of the Guenther family, which was built in 1859 and remains adjacent to the main plant, was lived in by family members until 1948. This beautiful historic home, which is listed in the National Register of Historic Places for its interior, was restored and opened to the public in 1988 and has become an award-winning restaurant, museum, banquet facility, and gift shop.

Giving back to the people who have patronized the company for so long is part of C.H. Guenther & Son Inc.'s heritage. The company supports initiatives and groups that better San Antonio's educational opportunities, culture, and community as a whole. In addition to scholarships for area students and children of employees, the company supports entities like the San Antonio Zoo, United Way, Goodwill Industries, Junior Achievement, and the Witte Museum to name a few.

As of 2011, a new corporate headquarters for C. H. Guenther & Son, Inc. was developing on Broadway. Upon completion, the former Butterkrust Bakery would be dubbed The Bakery on Broadway. In this location, C. H. Guenther & Son, Inc. will continue to grow its business and serve its customers in accordance to a strong, enterprising young man's dream from more than a century ago.

"To make money is not given to everyone. It is accomplished by those who are industrious, have a good insight into things and have natural wit and are willing to take a chance." ~ Carl Hilmar Guenther

ST. MARY'S UNIVERSITY

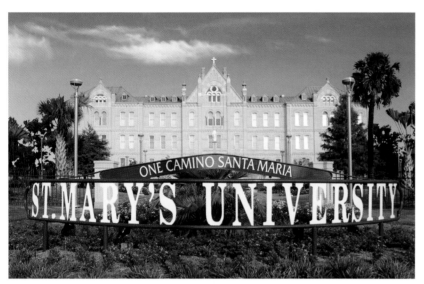

■ While the original site was along the San Antonio River in the city, today the university is located on a 135-acre campus northwest of downtown.

ST. MARY'S UNIVERSITY IS HOME for students intent on succeeding and where learning thrives in a culture that celebrates serving others. St. Mary's Institute, the foundation of Marianist education in San Antonio and the forerunner to St. Mary's University, was begun in 1852 by four Frenchmen who left their homeland to educate the youth of south Texas. With them, they brought the distinctive features and educational methods of the Society of Mary (Marianists), a religious teaching order dedicated to Mary that was founded by Blessed William Joseph Chaminade in the wake of the French Revolution.

Responding to the call of their superiors, they established St. Mary's — San Antonio's first institution of higher learning and the oldest Catholic university in Texas and the Southwest — to regenerate the people of the city.

The original cornerstones of the St. Mary's experience — academic excellence, service to community, and civic engagement — are enhanced by personal attention and robust academic programs that have made St. Mary's a nationally recognized liberal arts university. An all-male institution for 111 years, St. Mary's became fully coeducational in 1963.

WORLD CLASS ACADEMICS

For some 4,000 students of all faiths and backgrounds, St. Mary's provides a Catholic and Marianist education that promotes academic excellence while integrating liberal studies, professional preparation, and ethical commitment. The university's nearly 200 full-time faculty members, including numerous Fulbright Scholars and Piper Professor winners, teach in classrooms, labs, and abroad. Faculty at St. Mary's — 92 percent of whom hold doctoral or terminal degrees in their fields — are hands-on and committed to student success.

Tuition is priced below the national average for four-year private institutions, and St. Mary's provides students with many opportunities to maximize their investment by pursuing one of more than a dozen five-year combined bachelor's/master's degrees or the one-year MBA through the Graduate School. Additionally, there are eight combined master's/juris doctorate options, and an evening law program through the School of Law.

St. Mary's is a close-knit academic and spiritual community where students pursue studies in five schools offering 75 academic programs, including doctoral, law, and pre-professional programs.

■ With a student/faculty ratio of 13-to-1, St. Mary's small classes promote active learning.

The School of Humanities and Social Sciences is the largest, with more than 20 major programs of study, including International Relations, Political Science, English-Communication Arts, and Psychology. Pre-professional programs, such as health sciences offered through the School of Science, Engineering and Technology, attract students because of St. Mary's success in placing graduates in professional schools, and many students move directly into graduate and professional programs in other disciplines after completing their bachelor's degree. Several engineering programs are accredited by the Engineering Accreditation Commission of ABET.

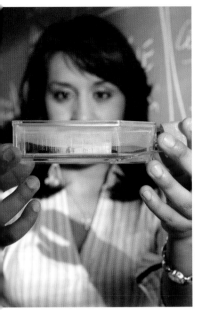

The Bill Greehey School of Business was the state's first Catholic AACSB-accredited business school. It consistently is ranked among the nation's top schools by The Princeton Review. The Greehey Scholars and E-Scholars programs provide students with personal and academic opportunities, while the school's trading room lets students manage a $1 million investment portfolio.

St. Mary's strives to produce graduates who understand cultural diversity and the interconnectedness of the world today, and its programs locally and globally break down barriers and build understanding. International opportunities include study abroad programs in England and Spain, as well as exchange programs in Asia, Mexico, South America, and Europe. Students also benefit from internships with companies such as AT&T, IBM, Microsoft, Pfizer, UNESCO, USAA, Valero Energy Corp., and "Big 4" accounting firms and government agencies.

Historically, more than half of graduates o apply are admitted to medical and ntal schools, well above the national erage of 35 percent.

St. Mary's graduation rates are among the state's highest, and the university has been designated by The Education Trust as a model of success for graduating Hispanics at the same rate as other students. Because of the quality and value of a St. Mary's education, the university consistently ranks high among top-tier institutions in the West in *U.S. News & World Report's* "Best Colleges" listings.

■ During the semi-annual Continuing the Heritage day of service, nearly 750 students, faculty, staff, and alumni volunteer some 3,800 hours of service at dozens of nonprofits throughout the community.

CO-CURRICULAR ENGAGEMENT

Whether writing for the award-winning *Rattler* student newspaper, playing on an intramural team, singing in the choir, volunteering at a homeless shelter, registering voters, or pledging a Greek organization, students can pick from more than 80 student organizations to develop leadership and life skills.

Service and civic engagement are central to the university's mission. Students give back to the San Antonio community and beyond through student organization service projects and through the Civic Engagement and Career Development Center's programming.

More than 70 percent of St. Mary's students participate in community service, logging nearly 150,000 volunteer hours annually. In 2010, *Washington Monthly* magazine, in its "College Rankings — What Can Colleges Do for the Country?" publication, ranked St. Mary's first in the nation for commitment to service, research, and social mobility. In 2011, The Carnegie Foundation for the Advancement of Teaching selected St. Mary's for the prestigious Community Engagement Classification, and St. Mary's has been named to The President's Higher Education Community Service Honor Roll since it began and, in 2011, received its coveted Presidential Award.

■ Interscholastic competition began in 1902 with baseball. In fact, in 1909, the school's team played an exhibition game on campus against the Ty Cobb-led Detroit Tigers.

With six national titles in basketball, baseball, softball, and golf, winning at St. Mary's is a testament to the spirit of competition and the tenacity and talent of student-athletes. Over the years, women's and men's teams at St. Mary's have won more than 100 conference championships and advanced to NAIA and NCAA Division II postseason play more than 50 times. The St. Mary's University Rattlers compete in NCAA Division II and in the Heartland Conference in baseball, softball, basketball, volleyball, golf, tennis, and cross country.

FROST BANK

■ Frost Bank and San Fernando Cathedral on Main Plaza in 1914, showing both horse and buggies and automobiles.

FROM ITS HUMBLE BEGINNINGS as a small family-owned mercantile store, Frost Bank has grown into one of the strongest mid-sized banking companies in the United States.

Frost was founded in 1868 by Col. T.C. Frost, a man of unimpeachable character and integrity who built his business around a belief in treating people with respect, providing service at a fair price, and employing sound business practices to keep his company safe. By staying true to its culture and founding principles, Frost grew into a statewide financial services company with more than 115 financial centers throughout Texas, offering banking, investments, and insurance. Today, Frost is one of 20 banks nationwide that comprise the KBW Bank Index, and its $18 billion holding company, Cullen/Frost Bankers, Inc., is traded on the New York Stock Exchange (NYSE: CFR).

Building a bank as strong as Frost is more than a quest to be the biggest; it's a responsibility to a legacy. Although corporate leadership has been in the capable hands of CEO Dick Evans since 1997, several members of the founding family are also involved in company leadership, and all are intent on handing a sound and solid company over to generations to come.

DOING WHAT'S BEST FOR THE CUSTOMER

While heritage is an important component of Frost's story, the only thing really old-fashioned at Frost is its impeccable customer service. At Frost, people — not machines — answer incoming phone calls. In its financial centers, bankers greet customers by name, providing solutions for life-cycle changes or help with other financial needs. Got a child heading off to college? Frost's personal bankers will talk about financing options long before tuition is due. Looking out for the next generation? Frost wealth advisors with trust and estate planning expertise can navigate the complexities of securing your assets for the future. Need help in creating a solid investment portfolio? A Frost professional will help you get your investments on track.

The experience of banking at Frost is, frankly, different. Rather than selling products, Frost focuses on offering solutions by listening to customers —both individuals and businesses — and staying attuned to their needs. As a result, the company develops products and services that make the experience of being a Frost customer better. For individuals, Frost's personal banking solutions range from checking, savings, and investments to online and mobile banking, credit cards, and loans. Frost wealth advisors offer investments, trust and estate planning, and investment advice for individuals. And its insurance experts provide custom-tailored life and health protection, as well as property and casualty coverage.

For the business owner, Frost offers a full array of financial solutions, with experienced commercial bankers offering the right financing options for a business to grow. From loans and equipment finance to treasury management solutions to improve cash flow and expertise in the needs of non-profit and health care organizations, Frost helps businesses succeed. Specialists can also help with asset management, tailored investment plans, and employee retirement plans. And Frost insurance professionals help business owners secure protection for themselves and their property, and employee benefits for their staff.

■ Customers can check their accounts online in the Frost Room at newer financial centers.

In every Frost location, employees share a culture that recognizes that everyone is significant. Customers can count on Frost to offer a square deal — excellence at a fair price — and Frost has a proven record as a safe, sound place to do business.

■ Frost founder Colonel T.C. Frost was a Confederate Army officer, a lawyer, and a Texas Ranger before opening a general store – and a bank.

GAINING STRENGTH IN ALL CYCLES

Frost didn't get to be one of the strongest mid-sized banks in the nation by making reckless decisions. Its leaders have always taken a conservative approach to banking. No exotic financing schemes, just safe, sound practices that mean a return for shareholders and a solid foundation on which customers can build wealth and a future.

During the 1980s, when Texas was in the depths of its own depression, Frost was the only survivor of the top ten banks in the state to stay intact without selling to an out-of-state institution or taking federal assistance. The bank has applied lessons learned during that time and has continued to grow, even through economic crisis and recession.

In 2000, Frost exited the residential mortgage business, opting instead to focus on services that reinforce the bank's relationship model. The decision kept Frost clear of the mortgage meltdown later in the decade. In 2008, Frost was the first bank in the nation to publicly turn down the government's Troubled Asset Relief Program (TARP) bailout funds because the bank was already on solid ground and did not need the assistance.

In fact, Frost has continued to add customers, locations, and technology while other banks struggle. In 2010, the company completed its $50 million Frost Technology Center, ensuring the capacity to meet future data and information technology needs as it continues to grow. This state-of-the-art facility enhances Frost's technological capabilities, including its online and mobile services.

BUILDING BETTER COMMUNITIES

Frost employs 3,900 people statewide, nearly 2,000 of whom are in San Antonio alone. Wherever there is a Frost financial center, there are people and resources committed to helping improve the local community.

Whether it's education, economic development, civic activities, health and human services, or culture and the arts, Frost is dedicated to making a difference. Frost believes its role is not only to serve the financial needs of a market area, but also to play a part in

Frost began building new concept locations the 1990s.

bettering the lives of its community. Funding decisions are made locally. After all, who better to make thoughtful decisions about charitable giving than those who see the needs first hand?

While the bank provides monetary support for a number of causes, employees offer their hands and hearts — independently and through the Frost A-Team Volunteer Corps — to mentor young people, support community celebrations, care for the sick and aging, raise awareness for charitable causes, and serve on the boards of local nonprofits.

There is a significant and recognizable difference in the experience of banking with Frost. Simply put, Frost is a bank that cares about your financial success.

TRINITY UNIVERSITY

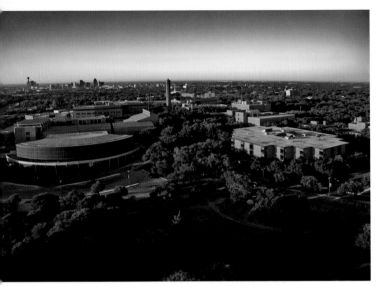

■ Located in the Monte Vista Historic District, the Trinity campus enjoys close proximity to downtown San Antonio and the many resources it offers Trinity students.

OVERLOOKING DOWNTOWN SAN ANTONIO, the Trinity University campus is beautiful and tranquil, an ideal setting for one of the most respected private, liberal arts institutions in the country. A closer look, however, reveals a bustling, cutting-edge university with a thriving connection to culturally rich San Antonio and a focus on global understanding.

ACADEMIC EXCELLENCE

Trinity attracts talented, motivated young people from across the United States and throughout the world. Most rank academically in the top 20 percent in their high schools, which combined with exceptional test scores and impressive personal achievements, prepares them for the rigorous academic standards they will face at Trinity.

Once on campus, opportunities abound for these young minds. With 41 majors and 55 minors, students pursue a diverse range of undergraduate and graduate fields, ranging from neuroscience to classical languages to accounting. Trinity students are ambitious and creatively use the university's abundant resources to enhance their knowledge and future marketability. Research programs, internships, and study abroad opportunities all serve to add depth and breadth to a student's academic portfolio.

True to its roots and core values, Trinity offers a flexible "common curriculum," grounded in the liberal arts with emphasis on writing, thinking, and problem solving. Ultimately, the goal of a Trinity education is to prepare a student for a lifetime of success in any endeavor. The university is proud to graduate critical and creative thinkers who will make an economic or social impact in their communities. Many begin this process through multiple service projects and other extracurricular activities as students.

At Trinity, high standards and expectations are also met with tremendous support. With a student-to-faculty ratio of 10-to-1, the institution provides students with an intimate learning environment rare in a university setting. Students benefit from access to distinguished professors — 97 percent of whom hold doctorate or terminal degrees — who also serve as dedicated advisors.

Trinity's emphasis on crossing traditional academic boundaries is at the core of the university's new $127 million Center for the Sciences and Innovation. The center is a 280,000-square-foot complex of glass walls that seeks to demystify the sciences, and classrooms and labs are designed to foster collaborative approaches to problem solving. Completion of the center is slated for 2014.

■ President Dennis Ahlburg joins students and faculty for the annual Martin Luther King Jr. march in downtown San Antonio, one of the nation's largest. Trinity students and faculty are known for their commitment to community service and involvement.

To promote excellence at every level, Trinity has invested in advanced digital resources throughout the campus and the sophisticated integration of these resources into the living and learning environment. Among these is the award-winning Coates Library, which supports thousands of digital databases, and a learning commons that works with students and faculty to implement effective teaching methods and learning technology.

A GLOBAL FOCUS

Trinity places a high priority on global literacy, incorporating an international focus on many levels. The goal is to prepare students to successfully live and work in a connected world.

With the Pacific Rim expected to play an increasingly greater economic role during the 21st century, the university created East Asian Studies at Trinity (EAST). This signature program includes one of the largest Chinese language programs in the country among liberal arts colleges. In addition to language, literature, and culture, the program encompasses East Asian religions, politics, and business as well as internships, exchange programs, and other opportunities to train future leaders to work successfully at home and abroad.

Trinity provides a bridge to the southern hemisphere through its unique Mexico, the Americas, and Spain (MAS) program, a multifaceted approach that fosters a deeper understanding of Latin America and Spain. MAS faculty from more than 30 disciplines train students on the language, culture, and other aspects of life in Spanish-speaking countries. Trinity's location in culturally rich San Antonio and the university's proximity to Mexico and other Latin American countries allows students in the MAS program to gain firsthand experience through internships, seminars, collaboration with foreign universities, and service learning trips.

Impressively, almost half of Trinity's students study abroad in more than 35 countries. However, global understanding also begins right on campus. With a student body of nearly 2,500 from 45 states and 64 countries, students live, study, and socialize together in Trinity's own version of a melting pot. Students also benefit from exposure to faculty who are leading experts in their fields and come to Trinity from all parts of the globe.

MIND AND BODY

Over 60 percent of Trinity's students are active in intramural or intercollegiate athletics, which underscores the university's support of personal development as a component of a well-rounded college experience. Over 30 percent of students compete as the Trinity Tigers in NCAA Division III intercollegiate activities, which consist of 18 varsity sports, nine each for men and women. The Tigers also compete in the Southern Collegiate Athletic Conference (SCAC), winning the President's Trophy for best overall sports record for 11 out of 15 years. Since joining the SCAC, Trinity has captured over 130 conference titles.

■ Beginning in 2014, all science and engineering classes will take place in the Center for the Sciences and Innovation. The 280,000-square-foot complex is designed to break down the boundaries among the sciences and propel Trinity students to the forefront of interdisciplinary research.

■ Trinity's enviable student faculty ratio of 10-to-1 ensures the close personal attention that is a hallmark of a Trinity education.

■ Trinity's award-winning Coates Library boasts a vast number of volumes, extensive digital databases, a learning commons, and the Trinity University Press offices as well as Java City, a popular coffee bar.

In a series of articles on college athletics in 2003, The *Wall Street Journal* noted, "Few of the 400+ DIII schools pull it off better than Trinity where learning and playing are in near perfect balance."

Trinity's achievements in sports go back many years, when the university competed in NCAA Division I athletics. The school maintains a particularly strong legacy in tennis, which includes a 1972 national team championship and individual Wimbledon champions, Chuck McKinley and Karen Hantze Susman, as well as three other Wimbledon title holders.

HUMBLE BEGINNINGS

In 1869, leaders in the regional Presbyterian community sought to create a "University of the Highest Order." With their vision and support, Trinity University opened its doors in Tehuacana, Texas, with just seven students. By the end of the first year, enrollment jumped to 100 as Trinity expanded its curriculum and doubled its faculty. As the university continued to establish itself and seek access to financial and cultural resources, it would move twice, once to Waxahachie, Texas in 1902 and ultimately to the Alamo City.

■ Although founded in 1869, Trinity moved to its current location in 1952, where famed Texas architect O'Neil Ford transformed an abandoned rock quarry into the distinctive red brick and lushly landscaped campus it is today.

Trinity's reputation for excellence caught the attention of San Antonio's Chamber of Commerce, which wanted to establish a Protestant institution for higher learning. On December 8, 1941, just one day after the attack on Pearl Harbor, the chamber kept to its mission and voted to invite Trinity administrators to meet. In 1942, Trinity merged with the University of San Antonio, using that institution's campus for almost ten years while enrollment climbed to 2,000.

The early 1950s brought another significant turning point — the development of a new campus that would facilitate the university's vision for academic excellence and growth. Renowned Texas architect O'Neil Ford designed the 117-acre campus, once a quarry, to feel like a "low-lying Italian village." From its landmark architectural features like Murchison Tower to the immaculate landscaping, Trinity is truly an oasis and the perfect setting for a premier educational institution.

PARTNERING WITH SAN ANTONIO

Although known for historic landmarks and cultural heritage, San Antonio is a forward-thinking city, and Trinity is proud to be a partner in its evolution. Trinity's Center for Educational Leadership is closely tied with San Antonio's reform efforts for grades K-12 in over 600 schools throughout the city. The effort brings together Trinity's resources with corporate and civic partners to improve schools in San Antonio.

President Dennis Ahlburg traveled to Asia in May 2011 to cement exchange relationships with several Asian universities, including Lingnan University in Hong Kong.

■ Participation in the Battle of Flowers Parade has become a popular tradition with Trinity alumni, seen here manning a 40-foot tiger balloon along the parade route.

■ Large Interior Form, a bronze sculpture by Sir Henry Moore, dominates the Coates Esplanade, which bisects the campus. It is one of several noted art works that embellish the campus.

Trinity's Urban Studies program connects leaders from city government, school districts, and social service agencies in efforts to revitalize sections of the nation's seventh largest city, both economically and socially. On a more grassroots level, Trinity students log approximately 20,000 volunteer hours at 25 local social service agencies, earning national recognition on the President's Higher Education Community Service Honor Roll. In addition, many of the faculty and staff serve on local non-profit boards or are engaged in other ways throughout the community.

Although students and faculty are active in the San Antonio community, Trinity also welcomes the public to share its extraordinary resources on campus including its concert halls, theaters, art gallery, and research library. Residents regularly attend The Trinity University Distinguished Lecture Series and the Cameron Lecture on Politics and Public Affairs, which draw nationally and internationally renowned speakers such as Colin Powell, Tony Blair, John Glenn, Desmond Tutu, Vicente Fox, and Madeleine Albright, to name a few.

TRINITY'S ECONOMIC IMPACT

Since relocating to San Antonio in the 1940s, Trinity continues to be an important economic engine for the city. With an annual operating budget of more than $128 million, the university employs approximately 700 local residents. It also attracts out-of-state and international students and faculty as well as visitors who spend time and money in the city, which has a positive impact on the local economy. Since 1980, Trinity has hosted over 100,000 visitors at more than 1,500 national and international conferences and programs held on campus. Professional associations, youth groups, and educational organizations select Trinity for its outstanding facilities and its vibrant host city, San Antonio, to hold conferences, trainings, and meetings.

Many Trinity graduates settle in San Antonio and launch very successful businesses, creating desirable jobs for people in the area. More recently, Trinity has proven to be a hotbed for technology entrepreneurs, such as the founders of Internet hosting giant Rackspace, who achieve international success, often while still undergraduates. Some of these start-ups have ranked in *Inc. Magazine's* 5000 Fastest-Growing Private Companies.

In summary, Trinity University is a dynamic chapter in a person's life journey — a place to pursue one's passion, collaborate across disciplines, develop critical-thinking skills, and prepare to thrive in a sophisticated global marketplace. It is no surprise that for two decades, *U.S. News and World Report* has ranked Trinity #1 among comprehensive universities in the western region of the country.

SAN ANTONIO WATER SYSTEM

■ A "purple pipe" and pump from a recycled water system located at a local high school that uses recycled water for its irrigation system.

FOR THE BETTER PART OF THREE CENTURIES, San Antonio has been nourished by crisp, cool water from the Edwards Aquifer. Today, San Antonio Water System is charged with securing and delivering diverse life-sustaining water supplies to more than a million people, as well as operating the city's massive wastewater and recycled water systems. The efforts of the utility have helped make San Antonio water's most resourceful city.

THEN AND NOW

Water from the aquifer feeds the springs where Native Americans encamped long before the Spanish established San Antonio in 1718. In the late 1870s, the city contracted with a local water supplier, eventually purchasing the water supply system and transferring its management to the city council-appointed City Water Board. In 1992, the council established San Antonio Water System (SAWS) to handle the community's many water issues.

Today, SAWS operates a massive system of pipes, water wells, pumps, storage tanks, and wastewater treatment facilities comprising more than 10,000 miles of water and sewer mains buried below its 560 square miles of service area. SAWS employs some 1,600 people, with crews working around the clock to ensure the reliable delivery of sustainable, affordable water services.

WATER CONSERVATION

Among the organization's priorities are efforts to reduce the city's reliance on the Edwards Aquifer. San Antonio is a nationally recognized leader in water conservation. Because the cheapest source of new water is water that is not

■ SAWS partnered to convert old washing machines into high-efficiency machines at a major downtown hotel as part of a commercial conservation project.

being used, SAWS offers programs that help homeowners and businesses identify opportunities to save water and money. Through a combination of educational resources and incentives for both residential and commercial customers, San Antonio is constantly looking for innovative ways to save water.

Through a free consultation with SAWS water conservation experts, homeowners can identify and fix leaks both inside and outside the home. SAWS also offers a water conservation audit to commercial customers along with rebates for water savings. Efforts like these have resulted in the city using the same amount of water today that it did 25 years ago, despite a 67 percent increase in customers.

AN ENVIRONMENTAL "TRIFECTA"

As part of its commitment to sustainable, affordable water services, San Antonio attempts to recycle and reuse nearly all of the waste products coming into its water recycling centers — turning wastewater into a valuable commodity. SAWS calls its efforts an environmental "trifecta" of recycled water, biosolids, and biogas.

As part of its commitment to sustainability, SAWS recycles and reuses waste products, partnering with a private company to treat and sell biogas (methane gas) on the commercial market.

SAWS manages the nation's largest direct recycled water program, which supplies about 115 million gallons a day of nonpotable water for commercial, industrial, and irrigation uses throughout the city. Recycled water that is not sold is released through the outfall at the Dos Rios Water Recycling Center into the river, providing critical flows to the upper San Antonio River and Salado Creek. Biosolids — the byproducts from treated wastewater — are used to generate compost for landscaping and gardening, which is sold commercially through area retailers.

Additionally, in the fall of 2010, San Antonio became the first city in the nation to partner with a private company to treat and sell biogas on the commercial gas market. Biogas — or methane gas — is a byproduct of the sewage treatment process. As biosolids are treated, methane gas is produced and usually flared off. However, SAWS partnered with a private company to capture, treat, and sell that gas on the market, getting a share of the profits in return.

MEETING DEMANDS

While much of the city's water still comes from the Edwards Aquifer, water is also drawn from sources such as Canyon Lake and the Trinity Aquifer. SAWS also has one of the nation's largest aquifer storage and recovery facilities. The Twin Oaks Aquifer Storage and Recovery facility is a large, underground reservoir where water is stored in times of plenty, and pumped back to the city for use during times of drought.

As part of its efforts to meet the city's water needs in the decades to come, and to reduce dependency on the Edwards Aquifer, SAWS continues to diversify and expand the community's water resources. The Regional Carrizo project involves drawing water from the Carrizo Aquifer in Gonzales County, some 50 miles away from the city. SAWS will rent available capacity in an existing pipeline to transport up to 13 million gallons of water per day to San Antonio.

Through the construction of its desalination plant, San Antonio expects to generate roughly 10 million gallons of water per day from the Wilcox Aquifer, treating brackish groundwater for use as drinking water.

COMMUNITY SUCCESS

Perhaps the most critical component of SAWS operations is public participation in operations and planning. Conservation is a success story because of the involvement and buy-in of the community. The people of San Antonio work together to conserve, an important factor during times of drought when following watering restrictions is so critical to meet required pumping cutbacks.

San Antonio continues to be recognized at the local, state, and national levels for excellence and integrity in water management, conservation, and innovative operations. SAWS remains committed to providing sustainable, affordable water services today and tomorrow for San Antonio and the surrounding communities. These efforts are what make San Antonio water's most resourceful city.

■ This large diameter pipe will be installed as part of an infrastructure improvement project.

OUR LADY OF THE LAKE UNIVERSITY

■ The main campus of Our Lady of the Lake University was established in 1895 on the west side of San Antonio on the banks of Lake Elmendorf.

Our Lady of the Lake University (OLLU) is a private, Catholic university that was founded in 1895 by the Congregation of Divine Providence. The university, nestled on a serene lakeside campus in San Antonio, takes great pride in instilling students with a strong sense of leadership and service.

The university has been federally designated as a Hispanic-Serving Institution and features the highest percentage of Hispanic students out of all private universities in the nation. Nearly 70 percent of undergraduate students and 50 percent of graduate students are of Hispanic descent. In addition, more than 70 percent of the student population is female.

"Service is a big component of who we are," says Anne Gomez, director of marketing and communications. "That's why we're so focused on serving first-generation college students, especially Mexican Americans, because they have traditionally been an underserved population."

In fact, nearly two-thirds of the university's students are the first members of their families to go to college. "The reason we're able to draw these types of students to us is that we put an academic program into place that provides them with the support and resources they need to succeed at this level," says Gomez, adding that, through its Higher Education for a New America initiative, OLLU shares its knowledge with other universities experiencing growing Hispanic enrollments. "As this population grows, we want to help reach them, teach them, and see them graduate."

Our Lady of the Lake offers 33 bachelor's degree programs, 14 master's degree programs, and two doctoral degree programs. With a student-to-faculty ratio of 15-to-1, classes are small and students are able receive the personalized education they need. More than three decades ago, OLLU also started the region's first weekend college program, which caters to working adults needing a flexible schedule in order to complete their degree or pursue graduate level studies. OLLU's programs range from the arts and sciences, cyber security, and Master of Business Administration to communication disorders, counseling psychology, social work, education, and leadership studies.

With more than 60 student organizations on campus and 12 intercollegiate athletic teams that participate in the National Association of Intercollegiate Athletics, students receive a very well-rounded experience.

Because service is such a crucial component of OLLU's heritage, all undergraduates are required to complete service-learning courses related to their degree in order to graduate. The benefits of this are twofold: students aid a person or organization in need while simultaneously learning valuable job skills.

■ The Main Building of Our Lady of the Lake University was completely renovated i 2010 and includes the latest in educational technology.

"Our students often think of the university as their family. There's a very close-knit feeling here," says Gomez. "Not only do we impact the student's life, we also impact the entire family because the student has now forged a path for other people in their family to earn a degree. After a first-generation student graduates, we'll often see their siblings and sometimes even their parents come here for their degrees. It can change an entire family."

WAYLAND BAPTIST UNIVERSITY

IN 1908, DR. JAMES HENRY WAYLAND, a physician in the Texas Panhandle, donated $10,000 and 25 acres of land to the city of Plainview to establish a faith-based school that would be open to all. With that, Wayland Baptist University was founded with the mission to "to educate students in an academically challenging, learning-focused and distinctively Christian environment for professional success, lifelong learning, and service to God and humankind."

More than 100 years later, Wayland Baptist University (WBU) has grown to become the fourth largest Baptist university in the United States. Wayland features 11 campuses worldwide with total enrollment approaching 7,000. While its central campus is located in Plainview, the university has additional Texas campuses in Amarillo, Lubbock, Wichita Falls, and San Antonio. Around the world, WBU campuses can be found in Albuquerque and Clovis, N.M.; Phoenix, Sierra Vista, and Tucson, Ariz.; Anchorage and Fairbanks, Alaska; Aiea, Hawaii; and Kenya, Africa.

"The model by which we've operated since the early 1900s is faith-based and open to all," says Executive Director and Dean of WBU San Antonio Dr. Jim Antenen. "And while we're a Christian-based school, there's no requirement to be a Christian to attend."

WBU's enrollment includes a very large military contingent. In fact, Wayland was one of the first universities in the country to tailor its programs around the specific educational needs of the men and women serving in the United States Armed Forces. In the early 1970s, WBU partnered with the U.S. Air Force to offer classes onsite at Sheppard Air Force Base. Following this model, Wayland continued to grow by establishing external campuses at other military bases around the country. Today, men and women from every branch of the armed services take classes at WBU.

In 1984, a 30-acre campus was established in the San Antonio metropolitan area, just off I-35 and O'Connor Road. While most students in and around San Antonio attend classes on the main campus, classes are also offered to military students at Lackland Air Force Base, Randolph Air Force Base, and Fort Sam Houston. In partnership with Alamo Colleges, WBU also offers classes at the Alamo University Center in Live Oak. Approximately 1,900 students are enrolled at the San Antonio campus, 45 percent of which are military personnel.

WBU offers a wide array of associate, bachelor and master degree programs, which were designed, by and large, to meet the needs of working adults and non-traditional students. "In many cases, students come to us already having more than 100 credit hours, but never managed to complete their degrees, which is especially true of the military folks," says Antenen. "So we developed the Bachelor of Applied Science program, which uses their current credits to help them complete their degree. About 80 percent of our students are enrolled in that degree completion program."

Most students attend classes in the evenings during the week or on Saturday mornings, but the traditional daytime programs, such as the Bachelor of Business Administration and Bachelor of Science in Interdisciplinary Studies, are rapidly becoming more popular. In 2007, WBU introduced its Bachelor of Science in Nursing program, which has grown exponentially since its inception.

A full array of graduate degree programs include the Master of Business Administration, Master of Arts in Management, Master of Arts in Religion, Master of Christian Ministry, Master of Arts in History, Master of Arts in Counseling, the flagship Master of Education program and the brand new Master of Science in Nursing program.

By offering more traditional degree programs, WBU now faces the unique challenge of having to expand its facilities and infrastructure in order to accommodate the greater influx of traditional students.

"We're growing by leaps and bounds, but these growing pains are a good problem to have!" says Antenen. "Our goal is to be recognized as the premier Baptist university for all of south Texas, and that our nursing and teacher education degrees become the programs of choice for the region."

WBU is well on its way to meeting this goal, thanks to its four core strengths: flexibility, affordably, quality education, and a friendly atmosphere. Students enjoy unparalleled flexibility with five convenient locations around San Antonio and a wide variety of class times, from 8:00 a.m. to 10:00 p.m., five nights a week. Several degree programs are even offered online, which allows students in the military, some of whom may be stationed overseas, to participate from across the globe.

Secondly, tuition at WBU is more affordable than you might think, sometimes costing only half as much as other programs.

Wayland's programs are regionally accredited and its faculty's academic credentials are impressive. In fact, the majority of its teachers work or have worked in their field of study, allowing them to bring their real-world experience into the classrooms. Classes are small, with an average size of only 19 students, so teachers are able to give students the personalized one-on-one attention they need.

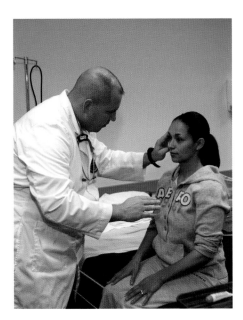

As a Christian-based school, the atmosphere is friendly and familial. The faculty and staff genuinely care about the success of students and take great pride in being able to make a difference. "Making a positive impact on a student's life is what we're all about," says Antenen. "Often, we have students who are the first in their entire family to go to school, which is something they never dreamt was possible, and now they're earning a bachelor's or master's degree.

"We graduate 600-700 students a year and many of them are mothers or grandmothers. They're setting an example for the rest of their family and it's an incredible experience to hear their families cheering for them. Nearly 90 percent of our students come to Wayland Baptist University because a friend or family member told them about us, which is a phenomenal testimonial. It really fills me with pride that we're able to make that kind of difference in a person's life."

UNIVERSITY HEALTH SYSTEM

■ The roots of University Health System date back to 1917 with the opening of the Robert B. Green Memorial Hospital.

COMMITTED TO CARING for the communities its serves, University Health System is a nationally recognized academic medical center bringing the latest advances in medicine to patients in San Antonio and south Texas.

Owned by the people of Bexar County, University Health System is anchored by University Hospital, a 498-bed acute care facility offering services for all ages, all stages of life.

While the hospital's comprehensive services address conditions ranging from kidney disorders, cancer, and orthopedics to diabetes, obstetrics, and urology, its signature services include organ transplantation, trauma services, cardiology, neonatal intensive care, and the neurosciences. University Hospital is home to the lead Level I Trauma Center in south Texas, serving a 22-county area that is home to some three million people. The center is the only hospital in San Antonio able to provide expert trauma care for critically injured and burned children. In addition, University Health System jointly owns San Antonio AirLIFE, a nationally recognized emergency medical transport program.

Beyond the hospital, University Hospital System is a network of outpatient clinics that provide varying levels of preventive health, primary, and specialty care. These outpatient clinics are designed to deliver services closer to home for the people of Bexar County and include the Robert B. Green Campus, a primary, specialty, and acute minor care facility. The campus also includes state-of-the art CT scan and MRI, onsite pharmacy services, and a wide range of rehabilitation services.

University Health System's roots date back to 1917 with the opening of the Robert B. Green Memorial Hospital. The hospital was jointly owned by the city and county and provided services to the indigent. From these humble beginnings, University Health System has grown into a comprehensive and nationally recognized academic medical center, in partnership with The University of Texas Health Science Center School of Medicine.

■ University Hospital is the lead Level I trauma center for Bexar County and all of South Texas.

The highest level of care is available in San Antonio because of the unwavering commitment of the Bexar County community. It was the people of Bexar County who, in 1955, voted overwhelmingly in favor of the creation of the Bexar County Hospital District and a property tax to support its mission to provide quality care to all, regardless of the ability to pay.

The new hospital district was essentially the Robert B. Green Hospital. But San Antonio was growing and, in 1968, the district opened one of the first hospitals in what is today the South Texas Medical Center. At the time, the medical center was mostly pastureland on the far northwest outskirts of town. San Antonio expanded far past the medical center and in all directions so, in the 1980s and 90s, University Health System leaders made a strategic decision to reach out to provide health care closer to home. Today, it provides services at about 20 locations across the community.

■ University Health System is in the top one percent of all U.S. hospitals for implementing electronic health records and advanced technology.

Still, San Antonio continued to grow and by 2008, University Hospital was too small to keep up with the growing demand. The organization's visionary leaders — the Bexar County Hospital District Board of Managers and its appointing body, the Bexar County Commissioners Court — recognized the critical need for expansion of care and resolved to make it happen. The $899.4 million Capital Improvement that resulted included a new 10-story tower at University Hospital and a new six-story clinical services building on the historic Robert B. Green Campus. It was the largest expansion program in Bexar County history.

These new spaces employ green design strategies to achieve energy savings, water efficiency, and reduced carbon dioxide emissions, demonstrating University Health System's commitment to being good stewards of the environment.

Named by U.S. News & World Report as the best overall hospital in San Antonio and one of the best in the nation for kidney and diabetes care, University Hospital is creating tomorrow's best practices today. Through the partnership with The UT Health Science Center School of Medicine's UT Medicine, patients in San Antonio have access to some of the top specialists in the nation, faculty physicians who are experts in their fields of specialization. These professionals bring a broad base of knowledge to bedside care through their ongoing studies and research into the latest techniques and most advanced medicines. The partnership with UT Medicine creates an academic environment that promotes a collaborative approach to medicine, allowing physicians to have a broader sense of knowledge through interaction with closely connected physicians, specialized nurses, and other health care colleagues. By working together, the physicians, nurses, and other health professionals at University Hospital are able to provide the most up-to-date answers for even the most complex medical problems.

As one of the Most Wired Hospitals and Health Systems in the nation, University Hospital employs the latest technologies available for diagnosis and treatment of medical conditions. Its advances include a state-of-the-art electronic medical records system, which allows physicians and health providers to stay connected whether making rounds or working from home. No more paper charts or X-ray film. With just the click of a mouse or a touch on a screen, the hospital's health professionals have access to the information they need to deliver the most accurate, expedient care.

■ The $899.4 million Capital Improvement Program includes a new 10-story tower at University Hospital in the Medical Center and a new 6-story clinical services building at the Robert B. Green Campus downtown.

The quality of care delivered by the professionals of University Health System stems from a sense of pride. In fact, a large number of employees have been with the hospital for decades. The organization has created vibrant and vital workplaces where those who entered health care to make a difference can truly feel there are achieving that goal. For many, it is the spirit of helping people from all walks of life that keeps them on board, the understanding that every new day brings the opportunity to provide aid to a member of the community regardless of their social or economical standing.

SACU (SAN ANTONIO FEDERAL CREDIT UNION)

■ SACU Main Office, a landmark on IH-10 West.

SACU (San Antonio Federal Credit Union) has handled its mission of service with care since 1935. "Our mission is to perpetually serve our membership," says Steve Hennigan, SACU president and CEO since January 2012. "Many generations of families have come through our doors. Some of our members came here with their grandparents when they were children, and now they come in with *their* grandchildren. Our spirit and culture are very different than those you'd typically find at a company of our size. We have a very warm, nourishing environment where our employees are concerned with helping members, the community, and each other. It's all about care and dignity."

Throughout its history, SACU also has been an innovator. Not only was it once the state's largest credit union, but it was also the first credit union in Texas to issue credit cards, the first credit union in the nation to offer an ATM, the first financial institution in Texas to offer off-site ATMs, and one of the nation's first to offer solar home improvement loans. SACU is also known in south Texas as the *Official Credit Union of the San Antonio Spurs.*

Twelve federal government workers pooled their money to form one of the first credit unions in San Antonio in 1935 and started a financial cooperative that has become a household name in San Antonio. Over the years, that credit union continued to grow and evolve, eventually becoming what is known today as San Antonio Federal Credit Union and referred to as "S-A-C-U."

One of the oldest and most respected credit unions in the country, with nearly $3 billion in assets, SACU has 18 locations throughout San Antonio, one location in Houston, and regional offices in San Antonio, Washington, North Carolina, Vermont, and Colorado that serve its manufactured housing financing division. SACU employs almost 700 people and provides a full range of products and services to more than 254,000 members.

A credit union is a not-for-profit cooperative owned by its members, not by stockholders. Unlike a bank, whose profits go to its stockholders, any profits that SACU gains are given back to its members in a variety of ways. This allows the credit union to provide low-cost rates for loans and lower-cost financial services that wouldn't otherwise be available. "The members of a credit union are people with a common bond," explains Jeff Farver, CEO of SACU for 21 years until his retirement in 2012. "They pool their money, which provides loans to other members. Members pay interest on the loans they take out and a portion of that money goes back to the depositors for letting them use that money. The money flow creates a financial ecosystem that is beneficial to both borrowers and savers."

Paige Ramsey-Palmer, corporate communications officer, adds that SACU is about helping people reach their financial goals. "We want

■ SACU Backpack Event – SACU and community partners provide backpacks and school supplies for children in need.

■ United Way Pacesetter Corporation – SACU proudly supports United Way in all the communities it serves, reaching 100 percent employee participation since 2006.

to help people who do not have access to financial building blocks for the seasons of their life," she says. "We aid people in managing their financial lives so that they can be in the position to reach their dreams."

SACU offers a wide array of products, such as checking and savings accounts, credit and debit cards, car and home loans, and IRAs and money market accounts. But perhaps the greatest differentiator is the friendly atmosphere and sincere level of personalized service. SACU's branches are evolving to become a social hub within the community, where members come in to chat with their favorite teller or other members and end up developing long-lasting relationships.

"Providing service that meets its members' individualized needs is the very core of what SACU does," says Farver. "SACU wants to serve its members in the way that works best for each of them, so it's important to really listen to what the members are saying. SACU's future is guided by what its members need and by meeting those needs in whatever way works best for each person."

A firm believer in helping its members and the community, SACU has never veered from its philosophy of "people helping people." One of the many ways SACU has done this is through its award-winning People Helping People lending program, which focuses on providing affordable housing solutions for people with low incomes. Since the early 1990s, SACU has partnered with several local organizations to provide citizens with the financial counseling, homeownership education, and low-cost loans necessary to access housing and become homeowners. Since its inception, SACU has invested more than $18 million in loans through these programs, giving San Antonio residents a real chance at achieving the American dream of owning their own home. SACU also supports the United Way, which provides a broad basis of help to a great number of members in the community.

"We don't give back to the communities we serve because we have to by law or regulation; we do it because it's at the core of who we are. Helping other people is the right thing to do," says Ramsey-Palmer. "Our employees have big hearts when it comes to volunteering in the communities we serve. They, in turn, are proud to work for a company that cares. Our average employee tenure is about 11 years, which reflects our care for employees and the community. This is quite rare for a company of our size. In addition, we've been selected as one of the best places to work in San Antonio for the past several years."

SACU also strives to be a good steward of the environment by offering home improvement loans to members who make improvements with solar power as an energy source, reducing the consumption of electricity.

"For more than 75 years, we have listened to our members. We have developed innovative ways to match savers and borrowers, helping those who depend on us reach their visions of success," says Hennigan. "Through our cooperative's contributions, we can help the communities we serve become vibrant, nurturing places for our credit union families to thrive and prosper."

■ National Public Lands Day sponsor – SACU has sponsored an official NPLD event since 2001, beautifying a public venue using volunteer labor and materials.

■ ExCEL Golden Apple – Since 1999, SACU has recognized excellence in public school education, presenting 19 teachers each year with a trophy and a check for $1,000.

■ Annual Shred Day – SACU provides free shredding of sensitive documents for the public to fight ID theft, encourage recycling, and lessen the burden on our landfills.

BROADWAY BANK

WHEN COLONEL CHARLES E. CHEEVER AND HIS WIFE, Elizabeth "Betty" Cheever founded Broadway Bank in 1941 with only five employees, around $60,000 in capital, and just $652,000 in assets, they envisioned a financial institution that would serve military families as well as residents and businesses throughout the San Antonio suburb of Alamo Heights. Today, their vision has grown to become the largest independently owned bank headquartered in San Antonio — a bank that has served generations of customers while holding true to its founding values of honesty and integrity, quality customer service, commitment to the community, teamwork, and performance excellence.

After all these years, Broadway Bank is still a family owned and operated company. Colonel Cheever's son, Charles E. Cheever, Jr., joined the bank in 1957 and continued to lead it for the next 40 years, along with Gregory Crane. Together, they would help get the bank through the hard-hitting recession in the late 1980s when many banks and savings institutions were forced to close their doors. Cheever Junior's son-in-law, James D. Goudge, became CEO in 1998 and maintains the bank's long-standing conservative philosophy that still helps the institution through hard-hitting times, such as the financial industry crisis that began in 2008. The bank is currently in its fourth generation of family ownership.

A BANK OF FIRSTS

Determination and creative leadership has made Broadway Bank an innovative frontrunner in the banking industry. The bank was the first to introduce many new services to the community. It was the first bank in San Antonio to offer mortgage lending, on-site discount brokerage service, off-site ATMs, and extended banking hours, the first to open a neighborhood convenience center, and the first suburban bank to open a downtown branch. The bank continues to develop new, inventive financial solutions to add to its vast array of personal, business, private, wealth management, and military banking services.

LASTING RELATIONSHIPS

What really sets Broadway Bank apart is its family atmosphere, community involvement, and its commitment to building lasting relationships with its customers. At Broadway Bank, customers receive personalized service and financial solutions tailored to their individual needs. Employees greet customers by name, give their children lollipops, and even offer their dogs biscuits. Most importantly, employees really listen to their customers' needs and work with them to create solutions. As a result, many generations of loyal customers and their families have made Broadway Bank their bank of choice for the past 70 years.

"Many of our customers have been coming here for quite a long time," says chairman and CEO, James D. Goudge. "They've helped us build the bank we are today. It truly is a relationship, and that's what we strive for — not just a financial relationship, but a personal relationship. We know our customers because they live in our community and because their kids go to school with our kids.

"We're here for the community. We owe our success to our customers, so we believe it's only right to give back. That philosophy dates all the way back to our founders and the guiding principles upon which the bank was originally founded, and it continues to permeate the way we do business today."

The philosophy extends to the employees as well. Goudge makes it a point to get to know each person and visits with departments and banking centers on a regular basis. The bank realizes the value that each individual brings, and it strives to provide them with the best benefits possible, including an employee-centric approach. As a result, employees voted Broadway Bank as one of the best places to work in San Antonio.

Colonel Charles E. Cheever, Sr., founder of Broadway Bank, summed it up best when he said, "If we take care of our customers and our employees, the numbers will take care of themselves."

BUILDING VIBRANT COMMUNITIES

Part of Broadway Bank's commitment to customers and employees includes helping to build strong and vibrant communities and improve quality of life through company and employee commitments of time, talents, and financial resources. By encouraging volunteerism, the bank's internal volunteer program, Care Corps, empowers employees to become leaders while building community awareness. Employees alone contribute more than 12,000 hours annually of their time to approximately 140 charitable projects. Goudge himself served as chairman of the Greater San Antonio Chamber of Commerce and has also served as chairman of Public Broadcasting Service television station KLRN Channel 9. "It's all about community — not just in San Antonio, but throughout south central Texas," Goudge explains.

A TRADITION OF STRENGTH

Through sound leadership and prudent decision making, Broadway Bank has become one of the largest, strongest, and best capitalized independent banks in the region, with 38 locations throughout south central Texas and on every military base in San Antonio. In fact, its growth required that the bank construct a new 80,000-square-foot, LEED-certified administrative building on its existing main campus. With more than $2.3 billion in assets and more than 650 employees, Broadway Bank's strength and stability have enabled it to survive and thrive, and it continues to earn the highest ratings from leading independent financial ratings services. That unparalleled strength, capital stability, and longevity give Broadway Bank a huge advantage over other financial institutions.

Courtesy of Clear Channel Outdoor, San Antonio. Richard Krudwig photographer

"We're here for the good of our customers, our employees, the community, and local businesses," says Goudge. "We are an independent and locally owned bank with a time-tested history of financial stability. With our financial strength and solidarity, we will continue to remain well capitalized and have a very solid foundation, even in times of economic turmoil. I can promise you that Broadway Bank is here to stay."

JEFFERSON BANK

JEFFERSON BANK IS A LOCALLY OWNED and operated bank serving the San Antonio, Boerne, and New Braunfels areas. The bank was founded in 1946, just after World War II, near Jefferson High School in San Antonio, Texas. Until then, there were no nearby banks in the fast-growing Jefferson area and the young citizens participating in the post-war economic growth desperately needed a financial institution they could trust to support their families and businesses.

A consortium of local business owners recognized the need for a bank, so they pooled their resources and created Jefferson Bank. The group hired A.J. Lewis, an attorney with the Texas Department of Banking, and Tom Murrah, an experienced Federal Deposit Insurance Corp. (FDIC) examiner, to lead the bank. When the founding group decided to sell the bank in 1951, Lewis and his wife, Grace, gathered all their assets and purchased the institution and Jefferson Bank has remained a family-owned company to this day.

■ Jefferson Bank at 1777 Northeast Loop 410

Despite its humble beginnings, Jefferson Bank has become an economic cornerstone for the community. Having started with just $125,000 in capital, the Lewis family and a group of dedicated, intelligent employees have grown that capital to more than $76 million, with another $900 million in assets. Jefferson has 11 banking centers throughout south Texas and employs more than 200 full-time employees. In 2010, Jefferson was listed among the top 10 percent best performing Subchapter S banks in the nation with assets between $500 million and $1 billion.

■ Jefferson Bank at 19002 Stone Oak Parkway

Jefferson Bank offers a wealth of personal banking products and services to help meet the financial needs of its constituents. Those products and services include checking and savings accounts, online banking, conventional fixed-rate mortgages, adjustable rate mortgages, Federal Housing Administration (FHA), Veterans Affairs (VA), home equity, remodeling, construction, portfolio, and other consumer loans.

The bank also supports local businesses with a bevy of business banking products and services, such as business loans, cash management, merchant services, and 1031 exchange service. Jefferson also features wealth management services, trust and real estate management, private banking and investment solutions. Personal and business insurance products are available through its subsidiary, Sanger & Altgelt, LLC.

"In the era of global banking, the people managing your money could be located across the country or across the world, but Jefferson Bank started as a neighborhood bank and we have banking centers located in the residential and small business communities within our own city," explains Paul McSween, president of Jefferson Bank. "We live here, we work here, and we serve here. We're big enough to help you maximize your earnings, while small enough to know you by name when you come into our banking centers."

With historically low rates available, Jefferson Bank is actively contributing to the local economic recovery by offering excellent mortgages to qualified individuals, families, and businesses.

■ Employee party celebrating Jefferson Bank's 65th anniversary.

"We're Americans actively participating in a global economy, but banking with Jefferson Bank is a more personal experience. Our businesses, our livelihoods and our families are local. No one can offer personal service like a locally owned, locally operated, community bank," says McSween. "The 200 plus employees here at Jefferson Bank are dedicated to offering that personal service to every account in our institution."

That emphasis on personalized service extends beyond the individual customer and into the surrounding community. In 2010, Jefferson's employees donated more than 3,500 hours of volunteer time to non-profit organizations, such as the March of Dimes, American Cancer Society, American Heart Association, Cancer Center Council, Christian Senior Services, Sunshine Cottage, San Antonio Children's Shelter, Girls Inc. of San Antonio, San Antonio Metropolitan Ministry, Children's Bereavement Center, YMCA, Junior Achievement, St. Peter-St. Joseph Children's Home, Seton Home, and House of Neighborly Service.

Providing the latest technology with traditional, customer-centric values, Jefferson Bank is constantly examining its operations for opportunities to manage its environmental impact and conserve resources. A recent example is the "Go Green Get Green" program, which offers a $10 deposit to customers who enroll in online e-statements, thereby reducing paper waste and conserving distribution resources. Jefferson took its commitment to the environment to the next level with its new Boerne Banking Center, which is Leadership in Energy and Environmental Design (LEED) certified and was designed with the current landscape of Boerne in mind.

Customers should be able to trust their financial institution to be solid, manage their assets intelligently, and understand that they are the bank's number one priority. Whether customers deal with the Jefferson Bank in the banking centers, over the phone, or online, they can rest assured that they are the most important asset that Jefferson Bank has.

"We believe that no one in the world can serve the people of south Texas like we can, and we bring that value to work every day," McSween says proudly. "At Jefferson Bank, our priority is earning long-term relationships through integrity, responsiveness, and commitment. This is personal to us."

■ Interior of Stone Oak Banking Center

McCOMBS ENTERPRISES

TEXAS IS A STATE OF LARGER-THAN-LIFE FIGURES, few more impressive than San Antonio's own Red McCombs.

Founder of Red McCombs Automotive, co-founder of Clear Channel Communications, namesake of the McCombs School of Business at the University of Texas at Austin and the Red and Charline McCombs Institute for the Early Detection and Treatment of Cancer in Houston, and former owner of the San Antonio Spurs, the Denver Nuggets, and the Minnesota Vikings, McCombs has owned nearly 400 businesses during his career and still puts in 60 hours each week at the family business, where three generations of McCombs are employed.

RED MCCOMBS AUTOMOTIVE

The McCombs empire started simply enough. Known as "Red" because of the color of his hair, Billy Joe McCombs was born 1927 in the small west Texas town of Spur. He attended Southwestern University, played football, had an Army tour of duty, then studied business and law at The University of Texas before landing a job selling cars in 1950 in Corpus Christi.

In 1958, McCombs and wife Charline moved to San Antonio where he formed a partnership in a Ford dealership. The store was the first of what would become a nationwide chain representing nearly every brand of vehicle, along with interests in

automotive import and distribution. In fact, in 1998, McCombs Automotive was ranked sixth in the nation for automobile sales, with more than 100 dealerships and revenues in excess of $1.7 billion.

The McCombs auto empire was built by a man of humble background who is renowned for his business acumen, charm, honesty, and integrity. Auto retailers nationwide employ a used car model pioneered by McCombs and his innovative aftermarket products and customer service divisions are viewed as industry standards. While his dealerships have each earned national recognition for sales and service, McCombs himself has been inducted into the National Automobile Dealers Association Hall of Fame.

Today the McCombs automotive enterprise employs approximately 1,000 professionals in San Antonio alone, and operations are overseen by a second generation, daughter Marsha Shields.

OIL & GAS, COMMUNICATIONS, REAL ESTATE, AND RANCHING

Never one to sit idle, McCombs' interests over time have encompassed other industries beyond automotive. His entry into the oil industry began in the 1950s, growing in scope during the 1960s when he formed a partnership with Oklahoma oil and gas producer Bill Forney and then delved into exploration and production. Together, they discovered numerous oil and gas fields and ultimately formed the Houston-based McCombs Energy, a nationally recognized oil and gas producer.

In 1972, McCombs and associate Lowry Mays formed Clear Channel Communications, which became publicly traded in 1984 and grew to become the largest global radio, television, and outdoor advertising business. The company is now privately owned.

Real estate is another McCombs interest. In 1997 he joined forces with Bart Koontz, forming Koontz McCombs to develop and acquire income-producing properties in San Antonio and beyond. In 2000, commercial construction services were added to the company's capabilities, and today the company has more than 5 million square feet of property in its portfolio.

McCombs' various properties range from apartments and office buildings to condominiums and resorts, including luxury resorts on Lake Travis and the Texas Gulf Coast.

Ranching is both a hobby and a business for McCombs, who raises and markets Texas Longhorn cattle and was the first to syndicate a Longhorn bull for $1 million. Red McCombs Ranches encompass thousands of acres in multiple states and operations include an elite breeding program and herds of both registered and commercial cattle.

AVID SPORTS FAN

As a man accustomed to winning in life, McCombs has always been a passionate fan of sports. At age 25, he purchased his first professional sports team, the Class B baseball team the Corpus Christi Clippers. In 1973, he formed the San Antonio Spurs, a National Basketball Association (NBA) team that has netted four national championship titles, and in 1982, he purchased another NBA team, the Denver Nuggets.

The jewel in McCombs' team ownership crown was his 1998 purchase of the Minnesota Vikings, a National Football League team that, under McCombs' ownership, went on to a 15-1 season and took the National Football Conference (NFC) Championship. In fact, during McCombs' tenure, the team went to the playoffs four times, took the NFC championship twice, and sold out the home stadium every game for seven straight seasons. Before he sold the team in 2005, McCombs was given the Owner of the Year Award by renowned quarterback turned FOX NFL Sunday analyst Terry Bradshaw, and received the Executive of the Year Award by Pro Football Weekly. McCombs is also the sole owner-recipient of the John Madden Thanksgiving Turkey Leg Award.

McCombs' interest in sports has never slowed. Today he is a primary force behind the new Formula One racetrack near Austin, Texas.

INVESTING IN ENTREPRENEURS

McCombs uses his own success as a springboard for others. Through McCombs Partners, he invests in talented people with smart ideas and companies on the verge of growth. In addition to an infusion of funds, McCombs Partners provides expertise and leadership, helping partner companies build their ventures into successful enterprises. Investments to date range from online programs and software to real estate and consumer lending to technology incubators and consumer packaged goods.

COMMUNITY PHILANTHROPY

Whether he is reading to students in schools, leading a charitable organization, or determining which worthy causes to fund, helping others comes naturally to McCombs. Every year, the McCombs family foundation gives monetarily to more than 300 charities that focus on youth, education, health, community, and faith. Substantial gifts by the foundation have also been made to the M.D. Anderson Cancer Center, Southwestern University, and the University of Texas at Austin, home of the acclaimed Red McCombs School of Business. These gifts are more than financial contributions, they are the legacy of a legendary Texan whose drive is paving the way for others to succeed.

WHATABURGER® RESTAURANTS

■ Founder, Harmon Dobson, in front of unit No. 1 in Corpus Christi, Texas.

WHEN HARMON DOBSON PLACED THE FIRST WHATABURGER on the grill in 1950, he didn't know that his small Corpus Christi burger stand would one day become one of the nation's most popular restaurant chains. That was 1950, and today Whataburger has grown to become a system of more than 720 locations across ten states.

BUILDING A BURGER LEGACY

Before founding the iconic Whataburger, the adventurous Dobson pulled a stint as a bush pilot and worked in jobs ranging from shipbuilding to oil drilling to diamond trading.

His first burger stand opened in a tiny portable building in Corpus Christi, where Dobson was intent on cooking up a different kind of burger — a made-to-order burger that tapped deep into the appetites of Texans — one so big and so fresh that when customers took a bite they'd exclaim, "What a burger!" Within the first week in business, Dobson sold 400 burgers and had patrons lining up around the block to get a taste of the 25-cent sandwich. Today, the chain that was named a Texas Treasure by the 77th Texas Legislature serves more than 460,000 customers in a single day.

Whataburgers are still cooked to-order, made with fresh, never-frozen beef, and served on toasted five-inch buns. Toppings can include everything from bacon and cheese to grilled onions and jalapenos to tomatoes and pickles, leading to estimates that there are more than 36,800 ways a customer can have a Whataburger.

Over time, Whataburger added other favorites to its menu, including its ever-popular chicken strips served with pepper cream gravy and Texas Toast. In 1979, a full breakfast menu was introduced to include favorites like Whataburger's delicious Taquitos, Breakfast On A Bun® sandwiches, cinnamon rolls, and pancakes.

In 2009, after reaching more than $1 billion in sales, the company looked further inland in search of a new home for its corporate office and chose a site in San Antonio — a city which was already home to 60 of the chain's restaurants. Today, Whataburger restaurants are favorite dining destinations for breakfast, lunch, dinner, and late-night meals, as most locations are open 24 hours a day, 364 days a year.

■ Whataburger Corporate Headquarters, San Antonio, Texas

■ Dobson gave his restaurant a name he hoped to hear customers say every time they took a bite of his made-to-order burgers: "What a burger!" Today's Whataburger is made just like the original, served on a toasted 5-inch bun.

A FAMILY KIND OF PLACE

Whataburger restaurants are all about family. The chain is still family owned and operated, with leadership taken over by Dobson's wife, Grace, upon his tragic death in 1967, and then handed over to the second generation, son Tom, in 1993. Tom's siblings, Lynne and Hugh are also involved in the business.

The people who work at Whataburger are known as Family Members, a title that helps create a culture of mutual loyalty, pride, and respect throughout the entire organization. More than 90 percent of the company's managers view their jobs as careers, and nearly half have been with the company more than five years.

Whataburger also fosters loyalty through a support system known as the Whataburger Family Foundation. Funded by weekly contributions from thousands of Family Members, the foundation's funds are available to help employees with emergencies or family crises.

The result of this family-style treatment is that folks who come in for a bite to eat — sometimes from many miles away — are also treated like family stopping in for a visit. There are plenty of stories to attest to the elevated level of service found at every Whataburger. For instance, a couple that stops in daily for lunch at one Whataburger restaurant is treated to a reserved table complete with settings. On a rainy day in Austin, another customer was greeted at his car by a Whataburger employee with an umbrella. Several couples have been engaged, married, or celebrated an anniversary at a Whataburger. Troops overseas, who have been known to receive Whataburger care packages complete with Fancy Ketchup tubs, frequently write to the chain to say how much they miss the taste of home.

A FUN KIND OF PLACE

With a name like Whataburger, you just know they're bound to have fun at work. Every two years, the company sponsors WhataGames, a company-wide burger Olympics designed to foster camaraderie and promote quality and service. The games consist of high-performing regional restaurant crews who compete for the title of WhataGames Gold Medalist along with a cash prize of $5,000 per team member. In all, WhataGames awards more than $140,000 in prize money to the top-performing restaurant teams in the company.

■ Photo of modern day Whataburger restaurant.

Whataburger also likes to give its customers a good time and recently did so by including them in the company's 60th birthday celebration with "Orange Night Out." This unique celebration included giving a free Whataburger to every customer who showed up dressed in the company's signature color as a "thank you" for their loyalty.

SELFLESS SPIRIT

As a company driven to serve others, a generous charitable giving program is a natural extension of the Whataburger culture.

■ Whataburger's gold medal team shows their pride at the finale of WhataGames 2011.

The company supports many nonprofit organizations across its geographic regions, providing monetary and in-kind donations, event sponsorship, and hands-on volunteers for charitable initiatives. Driven to make a difference, the company focuses its support in the areas of children's charities and education, persons dealing with cancer or disabilities, and programs that seek to prevent abuse or feed the hungry.

Whataburger also lends support to disaster relief programs, aiding neighbors dealing with the unexpected, and to military families by frequently hosting welcome-home events for troops returning from abroad.

Wherever it operates, Whataburger is solid proof that phenomenal results can be obtained from great ideas and a desire to serve.

SECURITY SERVICE
FEDERAL CREDIT UNION

■ Security Service Federal Credit Union volunteers work with Habitat for Humanity to build a home for a family in need.

EVEN WITH ITS RANKING AS TEXAS' LARGEST CREDIT UNION, Security Service Federal Credit Union enjoys a personal connection with each and every one of its members. "But it's really no surprise," says David E. Reynolds, president and chief executive officer, "because everyone we serve is a member."

While many understand the similarities between traditional banks and credit unions, there is a pivotal difference. "We're people helping people," Reynolds says. "As a not-for-profit organization, our members are our owners . . . there are no stakeholders beyond membership." The credit union isn't owned by a single person or a faceless corporation. It is owned by every person who opens an account . . . individuals from organizations and associations who, through their cooperative membership, help each other prosper.

HUMBLE BEGINNINGS, RETAINED VALUES

Founded in 1956 by eight determined men with $25 dollars in deposits, Security Service Federal Credit Union now thrives as the eighth largest credit union in the nation, and the largest in Texas and San Antonio, touting more than $6 billion in assets and employing some 1,500 people who serve more than 850,000 members.

Headquartered in San Antonio, Security Service was originally established at Kelly Air Force Base as a financial cooperative to serve the fiscal needs of the members of the U.S. Air Force Security Service Command and their families. Over time, the credit union opened its doors to individuals and other organizations by offering more than 2,300 ways to join. Eventually, the credit union expanded to 69 locations in Texas, Colorado, and Utah, always with a sense of longevity, sustainability, and community.

■ SSFCU is dedicated to instilling good financial habits in young people through its many-faceted education outreach program.

TOOLS FOR FINANCIAL SUCCESS

With clarity and a singular vision towards building strong financial futures for its members, Security Service uses a judicious approach in providing solutions and support. "Yes, we're conservative," says Reynolds, "but our strategic planning and careful decisions have helped us weather some rough storms over the last 55 years."

Key to this success is being able to stay in tune with member needs while discovering innovative ways to enhance their financial situations that are also convenient to access.

■ In addition to its youth education program, SSFCU offers a student-operated service center at Clark High School in San Antonio. Students are trained and supervised by SSFCU Member Service Representatives and handle transactions for fellow students, faculty, and staff at the school.

These solutions come in various forms. Security Service was one of the first credit unions in the country to offer online banking and auto lending at the point of purchase. A 24/7, award-winning member contact center yields a live person with every phone call who can help, regardless of the time of day or night, in English and Spanish. The credit union also has its own network of more than 100 ATMs and a co-op network of more than 28,000 throughout the country, service centers inside shopping malls with extended hours, and more than 4,200 shared branching locations nationwide. "Security Service is designed and built for efficiency, accessibility and proximity to where our members live and work, maximizing member satisfaction and convenience," says Reynolds.

A MEMBER OF THE COMMUNITY

While lauded as a financial services industry leader in size and market share, the credit union's internal measures of success include intangibles such as volunteerism and responsibility to the communities it serves. "Giving back to the community and making it better is part of our mission as employees, part of our core value system," says Reynolds. "It's a true reflection of our personal values."

The Security Service Volunteer Corps is a group of more than 780 employees who have donated more than 6,000 volunteer hours annually to charitable causes, such as Leukemia & Lymphoma Society (the credit union is a national partner), Christus Santa Rosa Children's Hospital, the American Heart Association, the American Red Cross, Habitat for Humanity, and many more. In 2010, employees boasted an impressive 97 percent participation in United Way giving.

■ Security Service Federal Credit Union operates 69 service centers in Texas, Colorado, and Utah.

■ Security Service is the largest credit union in San Antonio and the 8th largest in the nation.

Another way Security Service nourishes the community is by sowing the seeds of financial literacy. In addition to holding regular workshops for the general public and running a credit union at Clark High School in San Antonio that is overseen by Security Service staff but powered by students, a new project was initiated in 2011 with St. PJ's Home for Children. The Healing Garden Project, which was originally designed to aid young adults aging out of the foster care system by using a vegetable and herb garden to teach them financial and life skills, has grown into a way for all children at the home to learn about responsibility and healthy eating.

Superior services, state-of-the art technology and innovative financial tools designed to guide members in fiscal management — all amenities that place Security Service Federal Credit Union above the crowd. But ultimately, what sets this organization apart is the human factor. "Tumultuous times can test an institution's fortitude and the strength of its business planning. But Security Service — supported by the soundness of its member-centric mission, dedication of its caring employees, and counsel of its volunteer board of directors — continues to meet such challenges," says Reynolds. "We remain strong, steadily growing, and committed to helping our members achieve financial health and sustained well-being."

BROOKS CITY-BASE

IN A CLASS ALL ITS OWN, Brooks City-Base is a unique development offering tenants more than two million square feet of space amid a campus-like setting. Encompassing commercial, institutional, residential, and recreational space, Brooks City-Base is a mixed-use development with a sense of community where people can live, work, and enjoy a greater quality of life.

Brooks City-Base is located on the south side of San Antonio on the site of the former Brooks Air Force Base. Brooks City-Base was created through an Act of Congress and special legislation approved by the State of Texas, and conveyed by the United States Air Force to the Brooks Development Authority (BDA) in 2001. BDA was established by the City of San Antonio to own, operate, and redevelop the site into an economic hub and world-class center for research, technology, and business. BDA is governed by an 11-member board of directors appointed by the City Council of San Antonio.

The foresight of military and community leaders to create Brooks City-Base proved of even greater value when the 2005 Base Realignment and Closure Act moved military missions from the base. As a result, the vision for Brooks City-Base evolved to position the campus as an economic generator through the redevelopment of commercial and residential real estate.

RESEARCH AND BUSINESS OPPORTUNITIES

Research opportunities at Brooks City-Base stem from a long history of military innovation. From housing aviation pioneers and leaders to being a development site for life-saving techniques and scientific breakthroughs, Brooks has long been a place where great minds have thrived. Today, the 1,246-acre Brooks City-Base campus houses laboratory space, including two Level 3 bio labs along with nearly 400 acres of land available for built-to-suit development. These facilities are ideal for use by a wide range of industries, from bioscience and biomedical to health care and pharmaceutical to information technology and telecommunications.

In fact, 140 acres is designated for medical research and technology, with several acres housing the new Mission Trail Baptist Hospital and Medical Office Building, the DPT Laboratories pharmaceutical manufacturing facility, the Wyle ISE (Integrated Science and Engineering) Group, Bridge PTS, a campus of Texas A&M University, and the City/County Emergency Operations Center.

To support the dynamic business climate, the campus is surrounded by a vibrant retail sector that includes well-known big box stores, banks, restaurants, and other tenants. Moreover, the campus provides an ideal quality of the life offering residential housing opportunities.

UPGRADED INFRASTRUCTURE

Approximately $100 million is being invested in campus infrastructure improvements at Brooks City-Base.

For its current and future tenants, Brooks City-Base has already invested in a fiber implementation system with high-speed connectivity and reliable backup, storm drainage upgrades, and new detention/retention basins that have created eco-friendly ponds attracting hundreds of migrating birds. Roadway enhancements include improvements that accommodate the increased flow of traffic into the development, a three-lane collector street extension, a boulevard and other roads connecting the research area to external amenities, and connector roads to major highway loops. Construction also includes a signature gateway complete with landscaping and irrigation.

The campus also participates in a locally popular and highly efficient water recycling program that ensures a dependable water supply.

A PLACE TO CALL HOME

To make the former base a place where people want to call home, in 2011 construction began on a new $27 million multi-family development designed to offer high-end living options. The first phase of the 15-acre development, which is known as The Landings at Brooks City-Base, comprises 300 units that offer modern urban living. There are also 94 acres of the campus dedicated to indoor and outdoor physical fitness facilities and more than 180 acres is dedicated to green space and preservation, including paved pathways that encourage pedestrian traffic.

Recognizing the historic value of Brooks City-Base, the campus continues to house Hangar 9, the oldest wooden airplane hangar still in existence on a U.S. Air Force installation. The hangar and other historic structures on campus have been preserved through the efforts of the Brooks Heritage Foundation.

FINANCING AND INCENTIVES

As an entity under the guidance of the BDA, new business tenants have access to quick decisions, flexible opportunities, and customizable planning at Brooks City-Base.

A host of financing and incentive options are available to investors and include the City/County Joint Tax Phase-In Program, the Freeport Tax Exemption Incentive Program, Workforce Training Assistance, a Texas Enterprise Zone Designation, a Federal Empowerment Zone (EZ), and design-build and lease-back options.

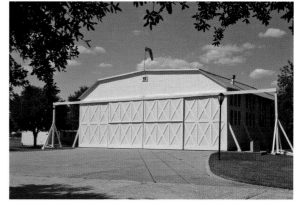

From its earliest days as a military installation to its current use as a premier business campus with ideal residential amenities, the location now known as Brooks City-Base continues to be a catalyst for economic growth on San Antonio's south side.

STA SAN ANTONIO

■ STA San Antonio Current 2011

SAN ANTONIO IS HOME TO A TEAM OF AVIATION PROFESSIONALS whose work keeps aircraft flying safely.

Those professionals are employed at STA San Antonio, a world-class provider of Maintenance, Repair, and Overhaul (MRO) services for cargo operators and commercial airlines. The company offers a comprehensive suite of services, including heavy maintenance, interior retrofit and reconfiguration, structural component repair and overhaul, and avionics upgrade services for a wide range of narrow-body, wide-body aircraft and regional jets.

Since commencing operations in 2002, STA San Antonio has steadily built a strong reputation by delivering high quality, on-time, and reliable aircraft maintenance and modification solutions. Equally important, it has also brought about long-term employment and income for some 1,200 employees and many supplier businesses in the region.

STA San Antonio reopened the facilities of what had been Dee Howard Aircraft Maintenance LP after that aircraft MRO company ran into economic problems. STA San Antonio quickly re-hired most of the Dee Howard Aircraft Maintenance workforce and has since grown the business substantially. Its complex of "big orange buildings" is a landmark at San Antonio International Airport, where STA San Antonio has more than 700,000 square feet of MRO operations under one roof.

Maintenance Planner Thomas A. Klimas, who had been with the Dee Howard Aircraft Maintenance for seven years before signing on with STA San Antonio, remembers that many employees were anxious when that company closed its doors. "But most of us stayed in San Antonio rather than look for work elsewhere because we felt confident that a new owner would recognize the capabilities and client familiarity that we would bring to the table."

That is exactly what happened and, with a talented and experienced crew on board as a core group, STA San Antonio was able to bring back a number of long-time clients and has never looked back.

CUSTOMER AND EMPLOYEE SATISFACTION

The company is fully dedicated to client and employee satisfaction. On the basis of this commitment, the STA San Antonio team drives single-mindedly to create value for their customers. The employees pride themselves on surpassing expectations to deliver on-time and quality products, and have received numerous awards and recognitions for their work and safety record.

Project Manager Marcos Villalon, who had eight years with the previous company before joining STA San Antonio in 2002, says the crew knows customers' operational needs and works to ensure that they are satisfied by delivering high quality and reliable work while minimizing aircraft downtime.

The working environment is what attracts many employees to STA San Antonio, Villalon says. It's a fast-paced workplace, where the staff is constantly applying new procedures and technologies to keep up with the never-ending need for safety, regulatory compliance, and high-quality, efficient performance. Many in the workforce have long tenure with the company and they treat one another like family, he says.

That special culture also draws many new employees to STA San Antonio from outside the city and they are quickly able to assimilate into the team.

Mechanics performing Winglet modification Boeing 757 aircraft.

■ NDT Technicians performing Engine Boroscope inspection.

■ A B757 undergoing heavy maintenance

UNCOMPROMISING STANDARDS

STA San Antonio is approved by the Federal Aviation Administration as a Class 4 Repair Station — a classification rarely awarded by the FAA — enabling the company to work on metal-skinned aircraft of any size and type. STA San Antonio's tight quality controls and procedures have also earned approvals from international airworthiness authorities such as the European Aviation Safety Agency and the Bermuda Department of Civil Aviation.

Production Control Supervisor Blanch Lawton, in the industry for 22 years before joining STA San Antonio in 2002, says the company's honesty and adherence to stringent standards has melded well with the work ethic already found in San Antonio. "In the eyes of aviation there is only one culture — do it and do it right," she says.

Safety is a top priority at STA San Antonio. From senior management to the mechanic on the hangar floor, safety is non-negotiable to ensure a safe and healthy workplace for all employees beyond the need for compliance with laws and regulations.

SPIRIT OF TEAMWORK, SPIRIT OF PRIDE

Composite Shop Lead Harvey Holmes, an industry veteran since 1961 who oversees several departments at STA San Antonio, says the people of STA San Antonio do whatever it takes to ensure that the job is done right. Purchasing Supervisor Sandy Wibracht, a 28-year industry veteran, says she enjoys the challenge of delivering each customer's aircraft on time, safely, and with superior results. And Project Manager Marvin Lane, who has been with STA San Antonio since the company's start in San Antonio, says work is performed with a high degree of enthusiasm as everyone is focused on the common goal of delivering to and beyond client expectations.

INVESTING IN THE COMMUNITY

With steady expansion, STA San Antonio — with its staff strength of 1,200 — has become one of San Antonio's major employers and the company strongly believes it has a role and responsibility to the community. STA San Antonio's success is linked with that of the city, and the company supports many local projects involving education, workforce development, and help for those in need.

■ Dee Howard in the 70s

When the opportunity arises, STA San Antonio contributes special volunteer resources and technical expertise, such as the restoration of an interactive aircraft display for the San Antonio Children's Museum. The company also assists and is involved with a number of local civic groups including the United Way, Future Farmers of America, Big Brothers Big Sisters, and the South Texas Blood & Tissue Center for which it participates in blood drives.

San Antonio and STA San Antonio — a winning combination for the aircraft industry, the workforce, and community vitality.

THE LYND COMPANY

FOUNDED IN 1980 BY MICHAEL LYND SR., The Lynd Company began as a full-service property management firm. It currently operates more than 110 properties with nearly 35,000 units across 16 states and in 50 different metropolitan areas.

■ The 29-story luxury apartment tower named EnV.

The company grew to its current scope of operations after second generation leaders, Michael J. Lynd Jr. and Adam David Lynd, joined the company in 1995 and 1997, respectively. Starting in 1995 with 1,100 units under management (more than half of which were owned by the Lynd family), the company ballooned to 15,000 units in the eight years to 2003.

In November 2003, Michael Jr. and David Lynd formed Lynd Residential Properties (LRP) as its multifamily acquisition arm along with partner Sam Kasparek, later adding additional partners William Jason Espejo and Sean Michael Kiehne. Shortly thereafter, the Lynd's formed Lynd Development Partners as their multifamily development arm and recently were awarded "High Rise of the Year" for an urban core development in Chicago. Through their investment and development activities, the Lynd principals have demonstrated their ability to source, acquire, operate, develop, and sell large volumes of multifamily assets.

The Lynd method to successful investing has always depended on using skilled acquisition professionals to cover targeted investment markets. The principals uncover opportunities through diligent market coverage, long-standing relationships, excellent acquisition reputation, and synergies from Lynd's vertically integrated management platform.

In 2009, Lynd continued to diversify into the commercial real estate space through its acquisition of a major stake in Easton & Associates, a Miami-based owner and manager of office and industrial properties throughout the southeast.

Since 2003, Lynd has acquired and/or developed over $1 billion worth of commercial and multifamily transactions. The bulk of these investments have been acquired with capital from four discretionary funds combined with co-investment capital from joint venture partners. To date, Lynd has harvested investments totaling $259.3 million in total value and realized gains of over $55.6 million on those dispositions while also delivering stable, consistent, quarterly cash flow distributions to its investors.

PRINCIPALS AND PARTNERS

Leaders of Lynd include Michael J. Lynd Jr., CEO and chief investment officer. Michael Lynd has structured the acquisition and financing of over $1 billion of multifamily acquisition and development projects, and has been an owner and operator of multifamily communities since graduating with degree in business administration with an emphasis on finance from Trinity University.

A. David Lynd, president and chief operating officer of Lynd, oversees an operation comprising over 1,000 employees and multiple offices including Miami, Houston, and Dallas. David Lynd also was responsible in forming Lynd's note acquisition and workout platform which acquired over $650 million in notes between 2010 and the end of 2011. David Lynd has also been involved as an owner and operator of multifamily communities since graduating with a business administration degree from Southern Methodist University.

■ David Lynd, President and COO

■ Michael Lynd, Jr., CEO and Chief Investment Officer

■ Samuel Kasparek, Managing Partner

■ Sean Kiehne, CFO

■ Jason Espejo, Senior Vice President

Samuel J. Kasparek, managing partner of The Lynd Company and principal in Lynd Residential Properties, oversees more than $250 million in annual revenues. In one four-year period, Kasparek oversaw a raise of more than $200 million in equity capital, which allowed Lynd enterprises to execute more than 50 real estate transactions. Kasparek has a Texas-issued certified public accountant's license and is a former Big 5 audit manager.

Jason Espejo is a partner and Sr. Vice President of Lynd. In addition to Espejo's primary role of presiding directly over the management operations, his additional responsibilities include proctoring the acquisition of assets through closing, reviewing ongoing performance, designing and implementing marketing and capital strategies, and facilitating the disposition of assets.

Sean M. Kiehne is a partner and chief financial officer of Lynd. Kiehne has had varying responsibilities with Lynd and has a Texas-issued certified public accountant's license. His background includes various senior accounting and financial positions with some of the world's largest employers.

A WORLD OF DIFFERENCE

Believing that the world is a better place when everyone contributes in some way, in 2004, the company branded its efforts to be a good corporate citizen as "A World of Difference."

Among the partners Lynd works with to improve the lives of others is Catholic Charities, Archdiocese of San Antonio, Inc., The Brighton School, Transplants for Children, and the United Nations Refugee Agency.

In addition to providing rental assistance to low-income families as part of its support of Brighton, The Center for Inclusive Communities, an organization that provides early childhood intervention and child development services for children with disabilities, Lynd has provided support to the leadership of Brighton and assisted the school in acquiring its San Antonio campus. Additionally, the company supports Brighton as the title sponsor of "The Taste of the Northside," an official fiesta event that serves as the school's major fundraising event. This event draws some 7,000 attendees and has raised as much as $300,000 in a single year.

The Lynd Company helps Brighton in its efforts to provide affordable housing for UNHCR, the United Nations Refugee Agency. The Lynd Company has waived application fees and deposits, adjusted rents when needed, and donated office space and units to aid refugees restarting their lives. For its efforts with the Refugee Resettlement Program, A. David Lynd was presented with a "For Your Commitment to Welcoming the Stranger Among Us" award.

Other activities over time have included helping victims of Hurricane Katrina, which hit the Gulf Coast in August 2005. In the wake of this devastating storm, Lynd helped evacuees with free rent, discount housing, employment, food, and basic necessities. These efforts demonstrate the commitment of Lynd to use its resources for the good of the community as a whole.

THE EMILY MORGAN HOTEL

WHEN PEOPLE THINK ABOUT SAN ANTONIO, the Alamo is often one of the first images that come to mind. Visitors travel from all over the world to experience the Alamo and soak up the history of the infamous 1836 battle between Mexican and American forces over Texas independence. And for travelers who wish to fully experience what the Alamo and San Antonio have to offer, lodging can be found adjacent to the historic site at The Emily Morgan Hotel, the official hotel of the Alamo.

Listed in the National Register of Historic Places, The Emily Morgan Hotel was originally constructed in 1924 as the cutting edge Medical Arts Building. In 1984, the building was converted into a hotel and named after the black indentured servant, Emily Morgan, who is credited for distracting and delaying Mexican Army General Antonio Lopez de Santa Anna during the Battle of San Jacinto, which led to a decisive victory for American forces.

"We're an amazing hotel for leisure travel and for anybody that truly wants to experience San Antonio," says General Manager Chris Johnson. "We're located directly across the street from the Alamo, so when you wake up in the morning, you're treated to a view of the sun rising over the Alamo grounds. With the River Walk just three blocks away, we're within walking distance from everything. But our hotel is preferable to a hotel you'd find along the River Walk, which tend to be loud and only offer nice views from the rooms that actually face the river. But you'll get great views of the city from every room in our building."

As one of the only hotels located on the original battlefield of the Alamo, guests at The Emily Morgan Hotel are able to experience living history.

"It's cool and exciting for me to be able to talk to our guests and share bits of history that they never knew," says Johnson. "For example, if you stand right here, you would have been right in the middle of Santa Anna's brigade during the battle. And Colonel Travis died about 30 yards from our front desk!

"We also have a lot of historic artifacts, like paintings of the battle and informative plaques on the walls. We have a really nice replica period gun collection above our fireplace and a core sample taken from a 1972 archeological dig of the Alamo. In all the world, it's the only piece of the shrine to have ever left the Alamo grounds, and it's right here on our front desk."

Thirteen stories tall with a brick exterior and a copper roof, The Emily Morgan Hotel is one of the most recognizable landmarks in San Antonio. Inside, the decor is what Johnson describes as "Modern Classic Legend" — contemporary with a Texas twist — complete with an old fashioned mail chute running from floor to floor.

Johnson also claims the building is haunted. Whether it is ghosts of fallen Texan soldiers, cats that Santa Anna's Army used as target practice, or former patients of the Medical Arts Building, guests sometimes claim they feel a ghostly presence or witness supernatural phenomena. Johnson says he hasn't seen any ghosts yet, but the hotel was featured on A&E's "Paranormal State" and Bravo's "Real Housewives of Orange County."

The Emily Morgan Hotel is pet-friendly and offers a variety of amenities, including a workout room, library, valet parking, and a stainless steel swimming pool with color changing lights. The hotel's restaurant and bar, Oro, features superb regional cuisine prepared by Chef Chris Cook, who is something of a culinary rock star. The Oro Margarita was recently selected as the "best margarita in all of San Antonio." Oro also features a monthly winemaker dinner and a Psychic Happy Hour every week, with complimentary palm readings, chair massages, and live music.

With three dedicated event managers and a wedding specialist on staff, the hotel offers 4,000 square feet of meeting space for business and social gatherings of up to 90 people. Events at the hotel are sophisticated and intimate, perfect for business meetings, corporate holiday parties, weddings, family reunions, and birthday parties. Clients work directly with the event managers to plan every detail and even meet with Chef Chris Cook to customize the catering menu, which ensures a completely personalized and interactive experience.

Designated by The Daughters of the Republic of Texas as the Official Hotel of the 175th Anniversary of the Battle of the Alamo, The Emily Morgan Hotel can also book business and social events on the Alamo grounds. The Alamo Hall can accommodate up to 130 people and larger events may be held outdoors on the lawn.

"As a AAA Four Diamond hotel, our guests receive a much more personalized experience than they would at one of the 'big gray box' hotel chains. Our service is individualized to meet the needs of each guest so that they receive a one of a kind experience," Johnson explains. "We have a lot of regular guests and they become members of The Emily Morgan family. They get to know us and we get to know them. When you stay at The Emily Morgan Hotel, you'll feel like you've experienced a bit of San Antonio history."

HAWTHORN SUITES – LIVE OAK VILLAS

WHETHER VISITING SAN ANTONIO for a day, a week, a month, or more, Hawthorn Suites/Live Oak Villas offers guests premiere accommodations and outstanding hospitality with all the amenities of home.

Whatever the reason for the trip — whether it's business, a family vacation, a long weekend, or stopping in as part of a group tour — the knowledgeable professionals at Hawthorn Suites know how to make guests feel right at home. Hawthorn Suites' highly experienced staff greets every guest with a smile, taking the time to explain the hotel's amenities, make suggestions for dining and entertainment in the surrounding area, or provide directions for any place in town. Even the hotel manager, Mike Neal, takes time to talk with guests in the Concierge Club Lounge during the complimentary social hour. A 30-year veteran of the hotel industry who holds the hospitality industry's premier credentials, Certified Hotel Administrator, Neal makes it his personal mission to ensure every guest is satisfied with their stay.

Ideal for extended stays in the San Antonio area, Hawthorn Suites/Live Oak Villas an all-suite hotel with spacious one- and two-bedroom suites that look more like apartments than hotel rooms. Every accommodation at Hawthorn Suites has two or more rooms, with separate living and sleeping areas. Living rooms are outfitted with a sofa or sofas, television with cable and premium channels, a working desk with ergonomic chair, and free high-speed Internet. Sleeping

rooms have king-sized beds with plush, pillow-topped mattresses and crisp white 250-thread-count linens, making it easy to get a good night's rest, and bathrooms feature soft towels and quality toiletries.

Hawthorn Suites also offers corporate apartments for the busy executive. Furnished or unfurnished, these rooms make it easy to get work done on the road. The hotel's business-friendly services include wake-up calls, faxes, free parking, local calls, and early check-in.

Other onsite extras include a fitness center with everything a traveler needs to work off the day's stress, and an outdoor heated swimming pool and hot tub for an afternoon in the sun or an evening soak. The hotel provides a complimentary newspaper each morning, helping guests on-the-go stay in-the-know. There is also valet service available as is an onsite guest laundry for those long vacations or business trips.

Feel like eating in or saving a buck or two? Every suite is designed with the convenience of an in-room wet bar kitchen or a fully equipped kitchen complete with stove, full-sized refrigerator, microwave, dinnerware, and utensils.

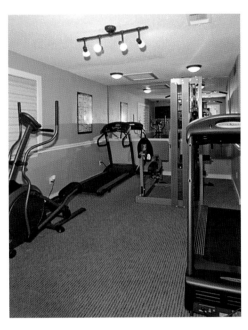

With its complimentary breakfast, mornings at Hawthorn Suites begin with a hot cup of coffee, tea, or cocoa along with favorites like bacon or sausage, scrambled eggs or omelets, and home fries or pancakes. The breakfast spread also includes a toast bar, with muffins, bagels, and pastries, and a selection of both hot and cold cereals. Fruit is always offered, varying by season, and drinks include fruit juices and milk.

Dining for breakfast, lunch, dinner, or a late-night snack can also be found at the wide variety of nearby eateries and convenience stores at places like The Forum at Olympia Parkway, a shopping mall offering a full complement of shops and cuisines.

Located at 13101 East Loop 1604 North, Hawthorn Suites is ideally situated near all the San Antonio has to offer. The hotel is an easy drive to any of San Antonio's largest employers, and whether it is SeaWorld San Antonio, Six Flags Fiesta Texas, the Alamo or Alamodome, the world famous San Antonio River Walk, or Schlitterbahn Waterpark, guests will find plenty to do when the working day is done.

Whether traveling for business or pleasure, Hawthorn Suites has the accommodations, amenities, and inviting staff to make any stay in San Antonio special.

CORNERSTONE CHURCH

■ Cornerstone Church Founders Senior Pastor John and Diana Hagee.

■ State-of-the-art Praise Center hosting Spanish Iglesia Cornerstone, Youth, and Young Adult services.

WHEN PASTOR JOHN HAGEE ARRIVED in San Antonio in 1966, he immediately set out to establish a church from which he could minister the Word of God to the local community. Founded with only six members, Trinity Church was the initial stepping stone to what would eventually become Cornerstone Church — one of the largest churches in America.

Today, the evangelical non-denominational Cornerstone Church has more than 20,000 active members hosting Sunday worship services at 8:30 a.m., 11:00 a.m., and 6:30 p.m. in its 5,000-seat sanctuary on Stone Oak Parkway. Church services are broadcast on more than 180 television stations and 50 radio stations reaching more than 100 million households across America and 245 nations worldwide.

"The growth of our church can largely be attributed to our core objective — to help every person who walks through the doors of our church at their point of need," says Pastor John Hagee. "Every Sunday, we have over 12,000 people who attend the three services and each person has a particular need; we seek out the need and meet it."

Despite its size, Cornerstone Church is a tightly knit community of believers. The church itself is made up of hundreds of home Bible study fellowships, which act as a support group to fellow members. Each week, Bible studies are held at the homes of trained church leaders. Members within the groups become personally acquainted and remain in constant contact, so when they attend church, they have a built-in relationship with their core group.

Not only does the church strive to meet the needs of its individual members, it also believes in the importance of reaching out to the local community.

One of the many outreaches of Cornerstone Church is through the Evangelistic Center on Donaldson Avenue. The Evangelistic Center feeds the hungry, clothes the needy, and provides counseling to the emotionally troubled.

Each year, the Center organizes neighborhood food drives and gives away hundreds of uniforms and backpacks filled with school supplies to low-income families. The Evangelistic Center sponsors GED classes, English classes, and bilingual Bible studies, and conducts worship services every Thursday evening.

In 1992, Cornerstone purchased the former Ursuline Academy Catholic Preparatory Girls High School, which was the beginning of Cornerstone Christian Schools. Today, the school features state-of-the-art educational facilities for both girls and boys, ranging from pre-kindergarten through 12th grade.

In the year 2000, Cornerstone acquired 210 acres in Tarpley, Texas, which has become the Cornerstone Conference and Retreat Center. The five-star facility houses, feeds, educates, and provides recreational facilities to several hundred people at a time.

The purpose of the Conference and Retreat Center is to enable Cornerstone's members to leave the distractions of daily life and better reflect on their relationships with family, friends, and ultimately with God.

■ Cornerstone Church, North Loop 1604 at Stone Oak Parkway.

Cornerstone constructed a 1,100-seat Praise Center in 2010, which serves as the educational, recreational, and praise center for its youth and young adult ministries as well as Iglesia Cornerstone which hosts services in Spanish every Sunday at 2:00 p.m.

The latest building project is known as The Ark, a state-of-the-art children's Sunday school educational facility, which will feature unique animatronics drawing the next generation into the House of God.

The reason Cornerstone Church feels like a large family is because it is. Like his grandfather and father before him, John Hagee is a fifth generation pastor, and his son, Matthew Hagee, is carrying on in his father's footsteps as executive pastor. John Hagee's wife, Diana, is the co-founder of Cornerstone Church and works alongside her husband, son, and daughter-in-law Kendal.

"It's very special for me to work every day with my family and many wonderful people who make this church and its outreach possible. We wouldn't be where we are today if it weren't for our dedicated staff and volunteers. We're very passionate about meeting the needs of our members and community and we believe in what we do," says John Hagee.

"When our members worship at Cornerstone we want them to return home with a message of inspiration, confidence, faith in God and themselves, and a hope for tomorrow that their lives will be rich and exciting because we love them and more importantly, God loves them. We want our members to 'Discover the Difference™' Christ can make in their lives."

■ Cornerstone Church Executive Pastor Matthew and Kendal Hagee

■ Sunday morning worship service at Cornerstone Church.

CORNERSTONE CHRISTIAN SCHOOLS

■ Cornerstone Christian Schools is a college preparatory school located at 4802 Vance Jackson in San Antonio, Texas.

■ The classrooms at Cornerstone Christian Schools have state-of-the-art technology, assuring each student's academic growth and development.

■ The arts are a key component of the co-curriculum plan at Cornerstone, which includes music, theatre and art.

CORNERSTONE CHRISTIAN SCHOOLS (CCS) is developing tomorrow's leaders today and believes that providing a top-quality education is the most important tool that can be provided to a child to help ensure a bright and prosperous future. Not only must that education include knowledge, it must also instill a sense of self-confidence, bestow the aptitude of leadership, and strengthen the student's relationship with God.

Cornerstone Christian Schools was founded in 1992 by Pastor John Hagee, when he procured the campus from the Sisters of Ursuline Academy. The academy was converted from a prominent Catholic preparatory girls' high school into a co-ed facility for pre-kindergarten through 12th grade students.

The beautiful 49-acre campus is located in the Castle Hills area of North San Antonio and has a current enrollment of nearly 800 students. CCS also provides a rapidly growing accredited online campus for grades three through 12 with students from around the world.

Dr. Jerry Eshleman, superintendent of Cornerstone Christian Schools states: "Most churches have ministry outreach programs, both domestically and internationally, which is exactly what Cornerstone Christian Schools is. Our schools are the largest ministry outreach of Cornerstone Church, both of which were founded by Pastor John Hagee. The church's invaluable support allows CCS to offer the very best resources to our students and faculty such as significant technology integration, cutting-edge computer labs, a theatre department with its own production studio, and science labs which mirror those found in large universities."

Cornerstone Christian Schools places a very clear emphasis on the growth and development of each student's Christian faith, both on an academic and spiritual level. Prayer is a daily occurrence, Chapel is held once a week, specific classes are dedicated to the study of the Bible, and the Bible's life-changing teachings are integrated throughout the curriculum.

Another characteristic that makes Cornerstone Christian Schools so unique is an extremely tight family structure. From the moment students enroll, families immediately connect with other children and parents.

Eshleman emphasizes, "Our school is a hub of family activity maintained by a variety of classes for parents and students alike including Rosetta Stone, self-paced computer classes, and parenting classes. We know that rearing children can be challenging at times so we do our utmost to be a strong support system for the whole family."

The education that students receive at Cornerstone is exceptional. Cornerstone Christian Schools either meets or exceeds the academic standards for the state of Texas and surpasses most of its colleagues in the private school sector. As a result, 100 percent of its students are able to attend a college or university.

"Education is a very competitive arena, but CCS ranks with the best of the best," says Eshleman. "The key to excellence is that we have the essential ingredients to produce an outstanding educational product. When it comes to our teaching staff, we have the very finest. Our faculty and academic administration average 18 years of educational experience. Many possess master's or doctorate degrees and some have taught as university professors. Our educators are very dedicated to the academic and spiritual investment that Cornerstone Christian Schools puts into each and every child."

Even though academics are foremost at Cornerstone Christian Schools, they are only a portion of what makes the school successful. In an effort to create well-rounded students, the school provides a full array of extracurricular activities such as student clubs and organizations, an award-winning fine arts program, and numerous sports programs. Cornerstone is proud to offer some of the finest athletic facilities in the state of Texas. Compared to the biggest and best public schools, Cornerstone's facilities are arguably second to none.

"When we declare that our school has an unprecedented standard of excellence, we mean it." says Eshleman. "We are always looking for unparalleled programs that are unique to our school. Our administration is sensitive to the fact that parents are making a choice to send their children to our school, as a result we do our utmost to surpass their expectations."

According to Eshleman, "The goal of Cornerstone Christian Schools is to provide an excellent education, which allows our students to feel absolutely confident that they are fully prepared with a strong foundation of knowledge, a greater leadership potential, and most importantly, a solid Christian worldview."

The mission statement of Cornerstone Christian Schools is to create and sustain a Christ-centered teaching-learning environment of unprecedented excellence designed to develop every student spiritually, intellectually, physically, and socially to their maximum potential.

■ Cornerstone Christian Schools educates students from grades K4 through 12.

■ The CCS Sports Complex is the home of the mighty Warriors. This impressive stadium helps to establish high standards in athletic competitions.

■ The Warriors at Cornerstone Christian Schools have won state championships in volleyball, basketball, soccer, and football. Cornerstone strives to have a broad-based athletic program of total excellence.

DOCUmation

WHEN COMPANIES NEED HELP with their office technology, they turn to DOCUmation. A business technology integration company, DOCUmation helps companies streamline their office document systems. Whether it is a copier, printer, fax machine, or document management software, DOCUmation's solutions help a company keep their operations at peak efficiency.

DOCUmation is more than simply a vendor of quality copiers and printers, it is a full-service solutions provider who partners with clients to find ways to operate more effectively while reducing expenses. "We really do take care of our customers, and one of the things we always want to do is provide the best service value in our industry," says Scott Woolfolk, president. "It's not just about the commodity of a copier or a printer, it's really about the value of that partnership to really look at ways to help our customers improve their business."

■ DOCUmation is one of the main sponsors for the UTSA Football Brute Squad tailgating events.

To provide answers, DOCUmation starts with a Business Technology Assessment, which involves a DOCUmation analyst team performing an office walk-through to determine what devices are being used, the volume of usage, and how everything integrates with back-office systems. After gathering the needed information, the DOCUmation team develops a plan for a new system that includes recommendations for changes in hardware, software, and processes that may be implemented. Still using a fax machine? DOCUmation can demonstrate how a centralized space on the network can help employees retrieve faxes electronically and save on paper, toner, and time. Have multiple models of printers, each using a different toner? DOCUmation can streamline the printer fleet to save time and money on supplies and supply management.

Started in 1997 with the merger of two office machine companies, DOCUmation now has offices throughout Texas in San Antonio, Austin, Dallas-Ft. Worth, Houston, College Station, Waco, Kerrville, and also in Denver, Colo. The company's growth can be attributed to a culture that truly cares about customer service. DOCUmation trains its staff to be master-certified technicians and certified document management specialists, then equips these professionals with the tools they need to provide solutions for customers, not just push the latest product on the market. "We want to provide, and we strive to provide, first-class service to our customers, and we go out of our way to make sure we have the best technicians on staff, so that we can provide truly a red-carpet, white-glove treatment," says Woolfolk.

Another factor helping earn DOCUmation an enviable record of 97 percent client retention is a unique acquisition strategy. Rather than follow the industry standard of offering restrictive, long-term leases to clients, DOCUmation offers a rental program for the equipment, making it easy for a growing company to change out its office machines as needed. No waiting for a lease to run out, clients can upgrade or downgrade equipment whenever the need arises and without paying an extra penalty.

■ DOCUmation is the host for the annual UTSA Football Signing Day Banquet.

Just as it wants its clients to succeed, DOCUmation also cares about the people it employs. In fact, this is a company where people want to work, as evidenced by employees repeatedly nominating the company as a *San Antonio Business Journal* Best Places to Work.

■ Tour de Cure 2009 SAG car drivers.

Caring about people also extends to a concern for community betterment, and DOCUmation is a company known for its giving spirit. "We believe that if you support your community, help your community to grow, it's going to enhance the overall well-being of San Antonio, and if we can make San Antonio a better place to live, and a better place to work, then that's going to come back to us in turn," says Woolfolk. "We may not be able to see it directly, but we'll see it indirectly. So anything we can do to help promote growth in San Antonio, help promote business in San Antonio, as well as take care of the people that are in need, that's part of what we want to do — it's the right thing to do. We're blessed to be able to help out with a number of different causes and we want to make sure we do our part."

DOCUmation is a major sponsor of the University of Texas at San Antonio athletics, providing the office technology and marketing needed for numerous sports. The company also supports Haven for Hope, an organization that provides education, job training, and behavioral health services for people who are homeless. By supporting the Any Baby Can organization, DOCUmation provides assistance to families of children with chronic diseases or health risks. The company also holds annual school supply drives and every Christmas, DOCUmation adopts more than 40 families, providing gifts and basic food supplies to get them through the season and into the new year.

DOCUmation also started a radio program called "San Antonio Movers and Shakers," which airs Saturdays at 10 a.m. on NewsTalk 930 KLUP. The program highlights people from San Antonio who are making a difference in the community. "It's not about our company at all," says Woolfolk, "it's really about promoting individuals in San Antonio that are from here and that have become important members of the community." The broadcasts are designed to demonstrate that anyone, regardless of socioeconomic standing, can make a difference in the world around them.

■ Tour de Cure 2010 DOCUmation Riding Team.

CORPORATE APARTMENT NETWORK

IMAGINE STEPPING ACROSS THE THRESHOLD of an elegantly appointed apartment complete with furniture, accessories, and household items — all personally chosen with your tastes in mind. Although you'll only reside in this apartment for a few weeks or months, it already feels like home.

Now compare this luxurious apartment to the typical extended-stay experience, one in which you're greeted by a sagging couch, mismatched dishware, and scratchy linens laundered past the point of comfort.

Most of us would take the first option. Wouldn't you?

In 1995, company founders combined their expertise in real estate and property management to create Corporate Apartment Network, a corporate apartment company based upon the ideals of Texas hospitality. Today, this family-owned and operated company offers spacious corporate apartments throughout San Antonio and across the nation.

PICTURE-PERFECT LIVING

Whether your needs require a fully furnished apartment near the airport, within walking distance of a downtown work project, or in a family-friendly area of the city, it takes just one call to Corporate Apartment Network. San Antonio-based owner Hope Sierra takes pride in making your furnished apartment needs a reality.

Gently nestled within high-end apartment communities throughout the beautiful city of San Antonio, Corporate Apartment Network has access to individual apartments that make the corporate housing transition a breeze. "Because we have properties all over San Antonio, we make sure the location is convenient for the client," says Sierra. "We are able to provide our residents with a place to stay close to a job project or where they are having a home built."

Each apartment complex is chosen for its A-plus rating, a designation offered by the San Antonio Apartment Association and based on a rubric of many features as well as the age of the property and area. Residential amenities including fitness centers, swimming pools, playgrounds, business centers, clubhouse facilities, and such, are major factors in selecting apartment communities as well.

Corporate Apartment Network so specifically meets the needs of its clientele that it can, for example, offer a one-bedroom apartment on the first floor of a complex close to a client's temporary work assignment, with an on-site swimming pool and state-of-the -art fitness center for after-work relaxation. Full-sized options include units with multiple bedrooms and bathrooms. All units include separate kitchen, bathroom, dining, and living areas. No space-stingy studios here, says Sierra.

Once the appropriate apartment is identified, Corporate Apartment Network secures a lease with the community and installs all utility services prior to the residents' move-in including electricity, cable, high-speed Internet, telephone, water, and trash. Particular pride is taken in customizing all of the apartments individually. Customized furniture and handpicked furnishings like flat-screen televisions, framed art, dinnerware, cooking utensils, and more, ensure everything is in picture-perfect order.

A TRADITION OF EXCELLENCE

While this may sound like exceptional care taken for just one client, it's not out of the ordinary. Corporate Apartment Network, with its team of network specialists, technicians, interior decorators, and customer service representatives, does the same for every new client, regardless of the length of stay.

"Our clients have the convenience to use Corporate Apartment Network on a long-term basis or on a flexible month-to-month status," says Sierra.

Sierra has been in the corporate housing industry for 27 years and says it's not the length of a client's stay that matters — it's the quality. "People aren't just an apartment number. I get to know them," she says, offering her personal mobile number so clients can reach her 24 hours a day, every day of the year — even holidays. "I want them to know they can speak with me, personally, and that I really want to know what the issue is — and that I'll make sure it's taken care of."

This attention to detail, as well as the company's willingness to accept pets in its corporate apartments, is just one of the many reasons most of its new customers are referred by previous clients. "Most of our business is word of mouth," Sierra says. "We believe the conveniences we offer are key to a pleasant transition — whether it's to a new job or a new home."

PORT SAN ANTONIO

A GROWING AEROSPACE PLATFORM

Port San Antonio is a 1,900-acre logistics-based aerospace and industrial master planned complex in San Antonio, Texas. The site encompasses much of the footprint of the former Kelly Air Force Base, which closed in 2001.

The Port is a specially created political subdivision of the State of Texas — established to take ownership of the property and oversee its redevelopment to ensure it remains a vital part of the regional economy. Over the past decade, Port San Antonio has attracted almost 80 organizations employing over 14,000 workers. It is one of the country's most successful base redevelopment efforts and helps generate over $4 billion in economic activity for the region annually.

■ Aerospace companies at Port San Antonio support military and commercial projects, including Boeing 787 Dreamliner planes undergoing change incorporation and refurbishment at Kelly Field.

Though created by government, the Port runs like a private business. It is operationally self-sustaining and earns its income from facilities it leases along with construction, property management, and other services it provides. It is the region's largest commercial real estate leasing and management firm and is ISO 9001:2008 certified in quality management. The Port oversees 12.9 million square feet of facilities and offers land sites ranging from 5 to 100 acres for build-to-suit options for existing and new customers, with a special focus toward aerospace, logistics, and governmental organizations.

The Port has three functional areas: Kelly Field, an industrial airport with one of the region's longest runways and one of the country's largest arrays of jet aircraft engine test cells; East Kelly Railport, a 350-acre site with logistics and manufacturing options with a switch not on the main lines and dual-rail access from BNSF Railway and Union Pacific Railroad; and mixed-use development sites in support of a growing workforce. The entire footprint is a designated foreign-trade zone (FTZ #80-10), which includes on-site U.S. Customs, an air cargo terminal, and quick access to Interstate Highways 10, 35, and 37.

■ Entrance to Kelly Field, where a growing number of companies are making the region a dynamic center for aerospace excellence.

From the outset, the aerospace industry has been the cornerstone of Port San Antonio's success. Between 1995 and 2001, when Kelly Air Force Base began a staged closure, the site's first private customers arrived, including Boeing, Lockheed Martin, Pratt & Whitney, StandardAero, and Chromalloy. These first tenants occupied millions of square feet of former Air Force hangar and workshop space at Kelly Field and were allowed to compete for maintenance, repair, and overhaul (MRO) contracts of military aircraft — seamlessly continuing the work previously conducted by the Air Force and laying the foundation that has attracted additional aerospace firms in the years since.

Today there are 14 aerospace-related businesses at the Port, directly employing more than 5,000 workers. As a result, the region is becoming a fast-growing national center for aircraft maintenance and manufacturing, with Port San Antonio helping lead the way along with partners that include the Greater San Antonio Chamber of Commerce; area institutions of higher education; and local, state, and federal officials.

■ Port San Antonio is a 1,900-acre logistics platform that supports a growing number of aerospace and other private and governmental customers.

In addition to delivering highly specialized facilities at Kelly Field, Port San Antonio has closely aligned its business strategies with those of its aerospace customers to ensure mutual growth.

For example, Port San Antonio has invested $350,000 in St. Philip's College, which operates a campus at the Port, to develop customized training programs for local aerospace workers, especially as commercial projects are added at Kelly Field.

Furthermore, as a political subdivision of the state, the Port can access government grants and special lending programs to conduct important capital improvements, including retrofits to hangars, ramp enhancements, and new infrastructure projects. The Texas Military Preparedness Commission's (TMPC) grant program, for instance, has provided almost $10 million to date to conduct upgrades to aeronautical facilities and ramp improvements.

Similarly, federal sources such as the American Recovery and Reinvestment Act of 2007 (ARRA), the U.S. Department of Commerce, and the Federal Highway Administration have helped fund important drainage and road construction work that facilitates business at Kelly Field.

These combined efforts have allowed anchor customers like Boeing and Lockheed Martin to flourish as they continue to provide military aircraft maintenance services and add commercial work, including the arrival of 787 Dreamliner and 747-8 air cargo freighter projects to Boeing's facility in 2011.

Additional industry icons to set up operations at Port San Antonio over the past decade include Pratt & Whitney, Chromalloy, and StandardAero. These companies work to support Boeing and Lockheed Martin and also undertake independent projects.

Furthermore, Port San Antonio is the headquarters of Gore Design Completions — North America's largest outfitter of custom aircraft interiors for wide body jets; they are the third largest such company in the world. The company began operations at Kelly Field in 2005 in a specially built hangar and has since almost doubled its facilities as demand for its specialized services continues to grow from customers worldwide.

To support aerospace growth, Port San Antonio has worked very closely with public officials to prepare new sites for additional aeronautical facilities. In 2012, completion of the 36th Street extension — a new road project into the heart of the property — will open 150 acres at Kelly Field to new development. The thoroughfare will allow for the extension of a taxiway and construction of additional hangars, workshops, and air cargo terminals able to accommodate up to 8,000 additional industry workers in that area of the airport alone.

■ Boeing's massive hangar against the San Antonio skyline. The building can accommodate 15 wide-body aircraft simultaneously.

BOEING COMPANY'S GLOBAL SERVICES & SUPPORT

The Boeing Company's Global Services & Support (GS&S) San Antonio business unit operates one of the largest military aircraft maintenance, repair, and overhaul (MRO) facilities in the world at Kelly Field.

The Boeing site was established in 1998 to provide an affordable, high-quality, short cycle-time maintenance and modification center for large aircraft. Under a lease through Port San Antonio, the Boeing GS&S San Antonio site has established itself as a high performance facility that has received national recognition for its achievements.

Boeing San Antonio continues the legacy of aviation as an anchor tenant for Port San Antonio. Boeing utilizes over 1.6 million square feet of enclosed area, including 940,000 square feet of hangar space along with 3.5 million square feet of aircraft ramps, run-up areas, and parking pads. The hub of site operations is Building 375, which is the largest free-standing, high-bay aircraft hangar in the world, and can accommodate up to 15 wide-body aircraft at a time. The current site capacity is 22 wide-body hangar positions and 33 narrow-body hangar positions.

Capabilities at the licensed Federal Aviation Administration Repair Station include facilities for paint and de-paint non-destructive inspection, drop-in maintenance, logistics support, and corrosion control, as well as back shops and office space.

After nearly 13 years as a military maintenance, overhaul, and repair center, Boeing San Antonio is now supporting commercial aviation. The first commercial aircraft, the 787 Dreamliner, arrived on March 4, 2011, for the site to perform change incorporation and refurbishment work. It was then followed by the 747-8 Freighter on May 11, 2011.

The Boeing facility's first aircraft, a C-17 Globemaster III, arrived for modification in August 1998. Maintenance and modification programs currently underway at the San Antonio facility include the C-17 Globemaster III Sustainment Partnership (GSP), the KC-135 Programmed Depot Maintenance (PDM), the KC-135 Global Air Traffic Management (GATM), the 787 Dreamliner Change Incorporation and Refurbishment, and the 747-8 Change Incorporation and Refurbishment.

Boeing's San Antonio workforce has an excellent performance record through the employment of Lean+ manufacturing and employee involvement. Customers continue to acknowledge, and even benchmark, strong program performance. Maintaining the viability of the Boeing San Antonio facility is in the best interests of Boeing customers, including the U.S. government, U.S. taxpayer, Boeing commercial airplanes, and our warfighters.

Boeing San Antonio has become a respected business leader in San Antonio, thanks in part to how the company uses its core competencies for a systems approach to citizenship that challenges it to constantly seek ways to channel its resources for greater impact. Boeing San Antonio has established community partnerships with The Children's Shelter, Morgan's Wonderland, Soldiers' Angels, the San Antonio Zoo, and Witte Museum to name a few.

Boeing provides over one-third of the aerospace products and parts manufacturing jobs in the San Antonio metropolitan area and currently employs approximately 2,800 people working on more than 40 U.S. Air Force airlift and tanker aircraft at any given time and one to four commercial aircraft. This work currently contributes approximately $360 million annually to the San Antonio region and State of Texas, with an estimated impact of $2.1 billion from present to 2013.

KELLY AVIATION CENTER - AN AFFILIATE OF LOCKHEED MARTIN CORPORATION

As one of Port San Antonio's anchor tenants, Kelly Aviation Center is Lockheed Martin Corporation's (LMC) only aircraft engine maintenance, repair, and overhaul (MRO) provider and serves as the company's shining star for public/private partnerships. Spawned out of BRAC closures, LMC and the U.S. Air Force (USAF) have teamed up to perform maintenance, repair and overhaul (MRO) on more than 2,000 engines at Port San Antonio, keeping legacy workhorses C-5s, C-130s, and P-3s in the air to support troops and humanitarian efforts around the globe.

■ Kelly Aviation Center's heritage of high-value performance for U.S. and international military aircraft began in 1999, when a BRAC closure created a public/private partnering opportunity between Lockheed Martin Corporation and the U.S. Air Force.

High production numbers coupled with repeatedly earning the USAF's highest performance rating have made Kelly Aviation Center the definitive example of how private industry and public entities

■ Kelly's nearly 1,200 employees and sub-contractors provide maintenance, repair, and overhaul services for seven different military and commercial aircraft engine lines.

can work together for the benefit of both. Kelly has perfected the model and, in 2010, decided to use the military business base as a foundation from which to enter the commercial engine market.

"We were able to capitalize on our many years of experience in the military arena by deciding to broaden our business base with commercial engines that derived from military engines," explains Chuck Artymovich, president of Kelly Aviation Center. "Some military engines have commercial applications, but the processes are completely different. Lockheed Martin has made a considerable investment so that we can maintain our service to the military and bring a substantial amount of commercial engine MRO work to San Antonio."

Port San Antonio has supported those efforts by making facility changes that are crucial to adding the capabilities Kelly needs in order to attract commercial business to include five new engine lines. The additional engine lines include the CFM56, which is the power plant for the 737 aircraft and allows Kelly to compete in the world's largest engine market, and the CF6-80 engine, which is flown on 747s, 767s, MD-11s, and C-5Ms. On the military side, Kelly is not only working to maintain its current capabilities, but to expand them. Already, Kelly has significantly increased its volume of building new F110 engines, which power fighter jets F-15s and F-16s, and other innovative teaming opportunities are being discussed.

"Clearly, our experience at Port San Antonio has been a very good one, a win-win for all concerned," says Artymovich. "We look forward to continue partnering with the Port so that Kelly is always positioned to serve as a strategic source for our military and as the MRO facility of choice for commercial customers, to bring in a steady stream of business to the region, and to provide high-paying jobs to the people of South Texas."

■ Four large engine turbofan cells plus four turboprop/turboshaft cells make the Test Cell complex at Kelly Aviation Center one of the largest independent facilities of its type in the U.S., providing almost unlimited capacity.

Chromalloy's San Antonio, Texas, gas turbine engine service and repair operation.

CHROMALLOY – LEADING TURBINE ENGINE SERVICE PROVIDER

Chromalloy partners with customers to deliver innovative solutions that reduce the operating expense and extend the life of gas turbine engines.

As the leading independent supplier of advanced repairs, coatings, and FAA-approved replacement parts for turbine airfoils and other critical engine components, Chromalloy serves commercial and military aircraft operators worldwide.

With more than 4,000 employees and sales and production operations in 17 countries, the company supplies components, coatings, and advanced manufacturing services to original equipment manufacturers, along with extensive engineering and component repair capability for commercial aviation, marine and land-based aero-derivative, and heavy industrial turbine engines.

Founded 60 years ago as a producer of protective coatings for turbine airfoils, Chromalloy has grown to become a leader in advanced service solutions.

Chromalloy's San Antonio operation has a strong legacy. The operation — a 292,000-square-foot repair and manufacturing center — is part of the company's global network of component repair centers, facilities and sales offices. It holds U.S. Air Force contracts as well as service contracts with major airlines and maintenance, repair, and overhaul (MRO) providers around the world.

The turbine engine operation at Port San Antonio was developed as a result of Chromalloy's participation as a member of the winning team on the Propulsion Business Area Contract in 1999, which contracted engine work formerly performed by Kelly Air Force Base.

Chromalloy offers a full range of services including design engineering, tooling, castings, machining, repairs, coatings and material solutions.

With the award of a 15-year TF39 military aircraft engine program contract, the operation secured its FAA repair station certificate in 2001 and entered the commercial market with CF6 component repairs that mirrored its TF39 repair capability.

Today the operation at 303 Industrial Park offers a full breadth of products and services for a wide variety of turbine engine cases and frames, combustors, rotating parts, and gearbox parts. And Chromalloy continues to develop turbine innovations for tomorrow.

Helping to train the next generation of aerospace technicians continues at Chromalloy. The company has partnered with aerospace companies and technical colleges in San Antonio on an internship program for aircraft mechanics and machinists.

Students in their junior and senior years in high school can test in and enter the program, and complete summer internships to prepare for employment as a mechanic, machinist or Non-Destructive Testing (NDT) technician.

Chromalloy has worked for decades with turbine engine operators in commercial aviation, the military, aeroderivative marine, and energy and power.

Chromalloy will continue to be driven by innovation — and continually strive to develop new and better turbine engine solutions for aircraft operators.

GORE DESIGN COMPLETIONS, LTD.

Gore Design Completions, Ltd. is a turnkey completion center specializing in aircraft interiors for dignitaries, heads-of-state, and VIPs. Founded as a design firm in 1988, Gore Design Completions (GDC) became an approved maintenance and completion facility for Boeing and Airbus — one of only two completion centers in the United States to carry this distinction.

Today GDC is the only completion center owned by designers, providing innovative solutions in aircraft design along with engineering, installation, and maintenance services for narrow and wide-body aircraft. The company's 280,000-square-foot hangar at Port San Antonio encompasses a custom upholstery shop, finish shop, machine shop, avionics/electrical shop, and full cabinet and sheet metal parts fabrication capabilities.

These all-inclusive facilities allow GDC to maintain total control over every project from the moment it arrives at the hangar until it is handed back over to the client. The company's hands-on approach has contributed to its reputation for delivering some of the finest quality in the industry.

An ISO 9001:AS 9100 certified operation, GDC uses three custom-engineered platforms to pre-fit airplane cabin furniture, minimizing downtime on aircraft that arrive at the hangar for work. GDC has also achieved Organization Designation Authorization (ODA) by the Federal Aviation Administration, allowing it to perform certification work on government aircraft.

GDC was co-founded by Jerry Gore and Kathy Gore-Walters, veterans of aviation design. Gore-Walters oversees an elite group of designers whose customized presentations include 3D renderings, animated interior walk-throughs, and samples of custom touches

such as china, crystal, flatware, and materials. Gore, meanwhile, is a former pro rodeo bull rider who turned to artistic design following a near-debilitating milling accident. Gore's responsibilities for other employers over time has included design for one of the industry's most complex and unique aircraft modifications of a Boeing 747-300 for a Saudi Arabian royal — valuable experience that served as a springboard when an industry downturn led to the formation of GDC.

Projects in the GDC portfolio include green completions, refurbishments, or maintenance for aircraft such as the Boeing 727, Boeing 737 BBJ, Boeing 767-300, Boeing 777-200LR, Boeing 757, and Boeing 777, along with the Airbus 320, Airbus 330, Airbus A340-200, and Airbus A340-500.

In 2009, as growth dictated the need for more space, GDC expanded its facility at Port San Antonio by more than 100,000 square feet, nearly half of which was an extension of the existing space to provide room for four wide bodies and one narrow body to be housed in the hangar at the same time.

STANDARDAERO SAN ANTONIO

■ "The Pit" today is a productive, visually appealing, world-class workflow system.

StandardAero San Antonio is the world's largest T56 engine maintenance, repair, and overhaul (MRO) facility, providing services for the Rolls Royce/Allison T56 turboprop, which powers the C-130 Hercules, P-3 Orion, and C-2 Cargo military aircraft. Opened in 1999 at Kelly Field, the StandardAero operation today encompasses over 400,000 square feet of production, warehouse, and office space, including indoor and outdoor engine test sites. StandardAero employs 570 personnel in San Antonio, providing world-class services for the U.S. Air Force, U.S. Navy, U.S. Coast Guard, and Department of Homeland Security. StandardAero's Government and Military Sector headquarters and Engineering Services Business Unit also reside at Port San Antonio.

StandardAero is known for Operational Excellence. As a result of the closure of Kelly AFB, StandardAero quickly and successfully converted the military MRO operation into a private-sector function, investing over $30 million to re-engineer and design the facilities for increased efficiency and specific performance parameters. The company retrained its workforce, and employees participated in and conducted the redesign of the processes throughout the facility. The redesigned facility enables StandardAero to operate at high levels of efficiency and process control, and to also realize additional benefits such as exceptional quality, new machining capabilities, low engine turn time, and high engine reliability. Most importantly, the upfront investment in equipment and training enables StandardAero to exceed customer expectations for delivery and quality resulting in "Excellent" performance evaluation ratings from its customers.

During the 18-month process redesign, there was no change or challenge that was considered too big to take on. For example, the entire facility is now designed in cellular layout, meaning small footprints of floor space (a cell) have been dedicated for the overhaul of a specific engine component or group of components. This cellular design eliminates the need to route components through multiple shops, thereby minimizing turn time, work in progress, and inventory.

The StandardAero facility is also unique in that it is a Zero Discharge Facility, meaning no wastewater leaves the facility through drains. Investment of $1.3 million in a Wastewater Treatment Plant enables StandardAero to reuse 85 percent of its industrial wastewater. The StandardAero facility has earned ISO 14001 Environmental Management System certification. It's a proud member of the U.S. EPA National Environmental Performance Track Program for environmental excellence. The San Antonio Water System (SAWS) recognized StandardAero with its Environmental Excellence Award for Performance and Conservation.

StandardAero San Antonio is part of a global service network of facilities throughout the U.S., Canada, Europe, Singapore, and Australia. Started in 1911, StandardAero celebrated its centennial year in business in 2011, marking a legacy of contributions to general and military aviation and a standard of excellence for which the company has come to be known.

■ Celebrating 10 years in San Antonio.

A PARTNER IN WORKFORCE DEVELOPMENT

■ St. Philip's College Southwest Campus is located at Port San Antonio—helping train new aerospace workers and updating the skills of the existing workforce to tackle new projects.

In keeping with Port San Antonio's approach of closely aligning its business priorities with those of its customers and providing comprehensive support, the organization has paid special attention to pressing workforce needs of aerospace businesses at the site. In the next few years, a substantial portion of aerospace workers nationwide will retire, and companies are urgently seeking new talent as worldwide demand for their products continues to grow.

One of the greatest resources at Port San Antonio is the on-site education and training programs provided by St. Philip's College, which is part of the region's Alamo Colleges.

St. Philip's operates a satellite campus at Port San Antonio that is a key training partner for Port customers. The institution provides education and training that enables the recruitment of new employees and ensures that current workers' skills are up to date.

The college has an established associate degree program in aerospace technology and also offers customized training programs. To date, Port San Antonio has invested $350,000 in St. Philip's for the delivery of specialized training programs, including those that focus on new commercial projects.

■ The Alamo Aerospace Academy is an important workforce training partner for the Port and its aerospace customers.

Furthermore, St. Philip's is the site of the The Alamo Aerospace Academy. Established in 2002, the Academy recruits talented high school students into a two-year hands-on program in aircraft structures and turbine engine mechanics. The advanced curriculum allows students to earn college credits during their last two years of high school and channels students toward paid summer internships with the Port's aerospace customers. Upon graduation, many of the students advance to promising careers in aerospace at Port San Antonio, often balancing their new jobs with continued higher education pursuits supported by their employers.

■ "Rebirth" by local artist Luis López, is a mural-size artwork celebrating the past, present, and future of the land that is today Port San Antonio, where generations of workers have built and repaired aircraft since the dawn of aviation.

TOYOTA MOTOR MANUFACTURING, TEXAS

■ The front lobby entrance to the plant

MOST PEOPLE KNOW TOYOTA as a Japanese company and as one of the leading car manufacturers in the United States, but what they may not realize is that Toyota is also a San Antonio company, employing thousands of hardworking Americans locally at its plant in south San Antonio.

In February 2003, Toyota made the announcement that it would be opening a facility in San Antonio that would produce the Tundra Pickup truck. The groundbreaking for Toyota Motor Manufacturing, Texas (Toyota Texas or TMMTX), occurred in October 2003 and the facility produced its first vehicle in November 2006.

The facility is located on 2,000 acres in south San Antonio and features nearly two million square feet of factory space. Toyota Texas employs more than 2,800 team members and the 21 on-site suppliers employ another 2,700 people, for a total of about 5,500 people working at the plant site.

TMMTX's approach to contributing to the community begins with its very own team members, which are the heart and soul of the company. In addition to excellent pay, team members also receive top-notch benefits. Toyota provides an on-site family health center for team members and their families, as well as suppliers and their families. The family health center includes primary care physicians, optical and dental care, physical therapy and radiology services, and a full-service pharmacy. The center receives more than 55,000 visits a year and employees have a very reasonable co-pay.

"The idea is to make health care readily available to be proactive in preventive medicine so that if somebody is beginning to show symptoms of any type of illness, they can be seen before it becomes chronic or worse," explains Craig Mullenbach, TMMTX external affairs manager. "This has been a huge benefit for the team members and their families."

When the market plummeted in 2008, many companies across the country went out of business or were forced to lay off the majority of their employees. Due to the lack of automobile sales, TMMTX halted all production for three months, but unlike other companies, Toyota Texas didn't let any of its permanent team members go. Instead of laying people off, Toyota Texas partnered with the city on a program called City Green, where Toyota took its team members out into the local neighborhoods to perform community service and beautification activities such as picking up trash and planting trees.

In addition to investing thousands of man-hours into the City Green project, Toyota Texas also reinvested in the training of its team members.

■ Team members helping to construct homes for Habitat for Humanity.

■ Team members perform landscaping at a community center for seniors.

■ Outside view of the Visitors and Education Center, where plant tours begin.

■ Aerial view of the plant site, encompassing 2,000 acres

In June of 2010, production of the Tacoma began on the same line with the Tundra bringing a more diverse line-up to TMMTX.

"We're always looking to participate and be engaged in the community," says Mullenbach. "Either through volunteer work, donations, or sponsorships, we work with more than 50 non-profits and schools districts each year. Halfway through 2011 alone, we were over 5,000 hours in company-sponsored community service." TMMTX's service in the community has been recognized by the United Way with the 2010 Volunteer of the Year Award for Large Corporate Organization.

Toyota Texas is heavily involved in the community through a number of volunteer programs. Partnering with SAMMinistries, Toyota is a title sponsor of an event called Street 2 Feet, which is a wellness program designed to engage the homeless in physical activity. The first annual run took place in 2010 and drew an attendance of nearly 800 people, raising nearly $60,000 for SAMMinistries.

Toyota Texas is also involved with various local chambers of commerce and has donated 32 trucks to different high schools in support of advanced automotive technology programs. Through a program that began in 2011, team members go out to local schools with tech and engineering programs to teach and mentor students in the basics of the Toyota Production System.

In response to the 2011 tsunami and earthquake in Japan, TMMTX and community partners, such as the Red Cross, put together a 5K run, which went around Toyota's plant site. More than 800 people attended the event and raised $40,000 for tsunami relief in Japan.

Being a good community partner extends to TMMTX's commitment to be a good steward of the environment. In San Antonio, water is a precious resource and at TMMTX all of the water used to support the manufacturing process is recycled water. This program accounts for 95 percent of all water used on-site and saves approximately 250 million gallons of fresh water per year.

Toyota Texas has received much praise for setting a positive example of how to be a good corporate citizen. The company has also received a number of J.D. Power awards, including the Silver Plant Award, for being the best in overall manufacturing quality for any plant in North or South America as well as a Gold Award for Best Initial Quality in the Full-Sized Pickup Segment.

Visitors may come and see the award-winning trucks and team members by joining one of the three free tours of the plant offered daily, Monday through Friday. The tours are open to the general public and reservations can be made through the company's website.

THE MADISON –
SAN ANTONIO RIVER WALK

NO LEASES. NO DEPOSITS. NO EXTRA CHARGES. These are the things that define convenience and make for remarkable luxury corporate housing at The Madison. A San Antonio gem, The Madison is a located in a peaceful residential setting less than two blocks — easy minutes away — from the renowned San Antonio River Walk.

The Madison's fully furnished condos and luxury corporate apartments offer all the amenities of an extended stay hotel with the privacy of your own separate apartment. A beautiful restoration of a classic historic property, The Madison was originally constructed in the early 1900s as housing for officers of the U.S. Army Depot Arsenal located just across the river. Now part of the King William Historic District, The Madison elegantly mirrors the grace and charm of its surroundings while providing guests a familiar sense of home.

Rooms here are designed for extended stays of a month or more and feature amenities not found in a traditional hotel room. From ultra-plush bedding and premium toiletries to fully equipped kitchenettes and in-room washers and dryers, The Madison envelops guests in a feeling of comfort and familiarity.

Whether it's a short-term project assignment, employment relocations, seasonal long-term getaways, or extended business trips, The Madison offers a temporary place to call home for people on the move: Busy professionals, homebuyers transitioning to new living arrangements, folks temporarily escaping the colder Northern climates, medical professionals, insurance claim adjusters, professional athletes, and workers in town with the Eagle Ford Shale project, especially prefer The Madison for its homelike feel and pristine, central location.

The Madison provides all the essentials for any length of stay, whether for 30 days or three years. Every unit at The Madison includes a high-speed, broadband Internet connection, along with Wi-Fi access throughout the property, flat-panel LCD televisions with premium movie channels, cookware and dining utensils, Sealy Posturepedic pillow top mattresses with superior linens, plus all the extras needed for everyday living.

Unit types at The Madison include studios and junior suites as well as one- and two-bedroom apartments. While studios contain kitchenettes complete with refrigerator, microwave, mini-convection oven, hot plate, and coffeemaker, junior suites have separate, fully equipped kitchens. Well-appointed one- and two-bedroom apartments have separate living areas, full kitchens with all appliances, a dining room, and in-room washer and dryer.

The property also has a wonderfully relaxing, private courtyard where guests often gather for drinks, barbecues, or just time to unwind.

The Madison is located at the corner of Madison and Beauregard in the King William Historic District of

Southtown, an area of San Antonio known for its fascinating mix of creative professionals and eclectic blend of historic homes and warehouses converted into shops, galleries, and restaurants. Activities nearby include horse-drawn carriage rides, concerts and music festivals, a 24-hour fitness center, and bicycle rentals for downtown tours or trips to destinations like the Alamo, the Mission District, the Witte Museum, the Majestic Theatre, and the San Antonio Museum of Art.

Guests of The Madison enjoy free on-street parking, and the property is just a short walk or trolley ride from the Henry B. Gonzalez Convention Center, the Rivercenter Mall, HemisFair Park, the Institute of Texan Cultures, and the Alamodome. The Madison is also just a short drive — only 15 minutes or so — to the city's largest employers including Fort Sam Houston and Lackland and Randolph Air Force Bases.

Stays at The Madison leave quite an impression. One guest, opting for a friend's recommendation other than the company-chosen "institutional housing," says, "Boy did I hit the jackpot! The Madison was situated in a quiet, charming area (very safe) with easy access to food and entertainment. It felt like I had my own condo."

Another guest, whose stay was a mix of business and pleasure, says The Madison was a perfect fit. "All the amenities without the hassle! . . . The big, deep tub was perfect for soaking each night after my long exploratory walks. The neighborhood is full of charm and has plenty of personality. Guest Services was available without seemingly, ever being present — perfect!"

Couples enjoy The Madison's charm. "We felt like residents of the historic throw-back (& quiet) King William District as opposed to visitors at a commercial establishment," says one couple, while another couple says if you want to see San Antonio without feeling like you're staying downtown, The Madison is a great way to go A third couple, who wanted something different, says The Madison fit the bill perfectly. "We . . . wanted something eclectic and off the beaten path . . . this was just the place. We loved that it was private and special. We were able to [either] walk to the River Walk area for dinner . . . [or could have] a wonderful Sunday brunch . . . next door."

The Madison is managed by Kings Property Services, offering skilled asset and facilities management services and inspections. Property management services offered include routine maintenance, renovation, cleaning and make-ready, and major repairs. Kings Property Services offers both traditional administrative services such as property promotion and advertising, tenant placement, credit and criminal screening, accounting and reporting, and collections and evictions along with various state-of-the-art web-based reporting tools. Kings Property Services is a leader in the property management industry with the use of sophisticated infrared camera technology to assist clients with developing the necessary supporting documentation concerning insurance claims, energy cost management strategies, and preventative maintenance planning.

HOTEL INDIGO AT THE ALAMO

■ The original lobby to the building has been 100 percent restored and preserved to the way it looked in 1909 when the building opened.

Hotel Indigo at the Alamo offers a unique experience to those on corporate travel or a weekend getaway. It is among San Antonio's newest hotels, yet one steeped in history. Not only do guests enjoy a premier view of Texas' most famous landmark, the hotel structure is located on the mission's original property and site of the 1836 battle.

Hotel Indigo also surprises guests with its own rich history. Back in 1909, railroad executive Colonel C.C. Gibbs spared no expense in constructing an office building with the best of everything — elegant architecture, elaborate mosaic floors, marble accents, the "modern conveniences" of hot and cold running water, and other impressive features.

Fast forward 100 years as the building is meticulously restored and transformed into a fully-functioning upscale hotel, which opened in 2010. The hotel's owners worked closely with the conservation society to maintain the building's original beauty and integrity, preserving the terrazzo floors, ornate light fixtures, mosaic tile floor with a "Gibbs 1909" motif, and other architectural features. Some of the original materials gained new life in the transformation. For example, marble and granite from an unused stairwell now serve as elegant tops for the hotel's front desk, bar, and dining tables.

A BOUTIQUE HOTEL

Hotel Indigo is an upscale line of boutique hotels launched by InterContinental Hotels Group. Each Hotel Indigo is unique and reflects the flavor of its particular locale. The concept is targeted to travelers who want something different, yet desire the conveniences and consistency of a brand hotel.

■ Guest Room

Hotel Indigo at the Alamo offers a distinctive blend of both old and new San Antonio. Set within the preserved 1909 building, the hotel's 91 guest rooms are attractively appointed with a modern southwest touch — colorful fabrics, quality wood furnishings, and restored hardwood floors. Contemporary design features are artfully incorporated throughout the lobby and common areas and in the 1909 Bar & Bistro and meeting facilities.

Well-seasoned travelers will appreciate Hotel Indigo's attention to their needs, including complimentary wireless high-speed Internet in rooms and common areas, 24-hour business and fitness centers, valet parking, and luxuries such as a spa-inspired shower in each room.

■ Exterior architecture on the building.

Located at the corner of Alamo and Houston Streets, Hotel Indigo is ideally situated — across from the Alamo, a short stroll to the River Walk, and a few blocks to the convention center. A trolley stop in front of the hotel transports guests to a host of other destinations around the city. Those visiting the city during the annual Fiesta San Antonio enjoy a prime vantage point for the festival's parades along Alamo Street.

Perhaps most distinctive, however, is the service culture at Hotel Indigo. Whether traveling alone or in a group, for business or for pleasure, each guest is treated to a level of personal service unmatched by traditional hotels. Hotel Indigo at the Alamo offers an inviting atmosphere, combined with its history and ideal location, to make every stay a memorable experience.

PHOTOGRAPHER PROFILES

RANDA BISHOP

Randa Bishop is a Las Vegas-based travel journalist and photographer. Her photographs have appeared in leading American and international magazines and newspapers from The Times of London to National Geographic Society publications. Her coffee table book, Las Vegas, Nevada – A Photographic Portrait was published recently, and her latest guidebook is CitySpots New York. She started out photographing spot news in the Big Apple, then concentrated on portraits for business magazines and feature stories for National Geographic World, covering wide-ranging subjects from solar-powered airplanes to children learning to be astronauts. After turning to travel photography, she covered over 60 countries and 50 islands worldwide, contributing to over two-dozen guidebooks. She is a member of Travel Journalists Guild and American Society of Media Photographers.

RUDY ORNELAS

Rudy has been a San Antonio-based freelance photographer since 1999. A graduate of State University of New York Empire State College in Manhattan, he specializes in urban photography, environmental portraits, and fashion. He also shoots events for clients around Texas and his work can be found in books, magazines, and gallery shows around the United States.

TIM THOMPSON

A freelance travel photographer for the past 35 years, shooting on all seven continents and in 75 countries. Based in Seattle, Thompson has published his work in many of the world's best known travel publications, including National Geographic Magazine, National Geographic Traveler, and Travel & Leisure. He has also completed seven single photographer books on topics as diverse as the Alps, Ireland, the Pacific Coast, and the Puget Sound region.

CARRIE YONLEY

As an avid photographer and lover of the outdoors, Carrie has recorded the natural world around her for decades. In her day-to-day life, and during her widespread travels and adventures, she has produced an extensive library of images from across America, capturing the spirit of the moment — of the light, the mood, the texture. In her portfolio, she showcases the diversity of our land — landscapes from the intimate to the panoramic, delicate Ozarkian flora, majestic images of the West, abstractions of color and light, and the character of American cities and towns, with dramatic cityscapes being one of her hallmarks. Carrie's work has been published in a number of coffee table books, and is used in offices and by business in literature and exhibits. Carrie exhibits in local art establishments at home in mid-Missouri, and she has been recognized in juried competitions.

INDEX